"*Anyone wishing to explore a uniquely interesting, highly relevant approach to problems common to us all, will find much to stimulate their senses in this unusual and fascinating book. Many techniques are original and engaging. This book is an intensely personal, philosophical construct which should be of huge interest to a wide audience.*"
Dr Herb Etkin, fellow of the Royal College of Psychiatrists, formerly Medical Director Ticehurst House Hospital and Counsellor to Eton College

"*A wonderful intensive read very interestingly presented and a fascinating take on the meaning of life. The book takes a simple premise and develops it into a deep, meaningful and thought-provoking ideal.*"
Stephanie Saunders, Lecturer and Fellow of the Society of Orthopaedic Medicine

"*Mr Bieber has tackled the most 'tricky' subject on earth in an imaginative and thought provoking way, embracing original concepts such as the Supreme Sense and the Speechless Real in an original and engaging manner.*

Most importantly he has grasped the nettle of the primitive, instinctual and reflex pattern of human emotions, their consequences (in particular the potentially destructive consequences of fear) and their protective genetic purpose. His review of the playground arena could not be more apt or topical."
Bruce Mauleverer QC, Patron, International Law Association

"*Am i loved? examines, explains, and empowers the reader by answering The Big Question in a serious and thoughtful way.*"
Don Luciano, TV producer and magazine editor, including Vanity Fair

Endorsements from anonymous readers selected at random in New York

'This book really shakes the tree in that you don't only feel like you've been enlightened, you feel educated. You feel like whether you believe some of it, all of it, or none of it – this is the truth as the writer sees it. This is a rare book.'
Male, 30's

'I made a point to look at the world through the lens of his words for a week and you know what? He has a point of view that should be heard and shared.'
Female, 20's

'Am i loved? shares a valid and interesting point of view. I would say argument but the book is written so beautifully there is no desire to convince people. A significant book.'
Male, 50's

'Even though I wasn't looking for a new philosophy, am not at all religious, or give life's meaning any thought, this book opened my eyes to things I didn't think I cared about.'
Female, 30's

'It's extremely well written, to the point if you want to put it down you are grateful to be reading something written so well you keep on going. I don't feel duped by this author. There are so many "gurus" who intend to make a living off what they spew. This author seems to have no agenda other than to share what he believes.'
Male, 40's

'This book made me feel good – like life really has a purpose.'
Female, 40's

For Dear Jolly,

with All Best Wishes

John

March 2021

Am i LOVED?

The most asked question of all time

John D Bieber

UMBRIA PRESS

Umbria Press
London SW15 5DP
alan@umbria press.co.uk

Printed and bound in Poland by Totem
www.totem.com

Hardback ISBN: 978 1 910074 25 1
Ebook ISBN: 978 1 910074 40 4

You are
The me of me
The thee of me
The we of me
The be of me
You are

To Joey my wife,
the greatest love of my life

Contents

Preface

'Subdue your appetites, my dears, and you've conquered human nature.'

CHARLES DICKENS (1812–70)

Nicholas Nickleby (1839)

L ove is passion. Love is life, joy, fulfilment. But I've seen love dying. I've seen love dead.

Love: the magic thread in the human tapestry, the sliver of warmth and light in a dark, cold world. Love: the single thing that every human being longs for, that everyone alive on this planet absolutely needs. Yes, love: the glue that binds two people, the bond uniting families and friends, the single force that fuels all human coupling, affording grace to individual existence. I've witnessed love, experienced love and been deeply blessed with love in my personal life, but as a lawyer handling divorce I've seen what happens when it's gone, lost forever like a dream that flies away.

With love extinguished, perfectly good and reasonable people fall victim to feelings they've never had or imagined before. Things become ugly, tragic and distressing, rendering them incapable of navigating procedures based on rights and entitlements. They are simply too in thrall to their emotions to see the wood for the trees.

This is what prompted me to write this book explaining the human condition. Because I wanted to bring understanding to things we plainly do not understand. I wanted to offer the chance to enhance the quality of our lives. My conclusions shed new light on all aspects of human experience. Suddenly our lives make sense and our previous understandings seem wrong, for we can see now how we have been engineered and why, how we are intended to function and how we have previously got everything wrong.

In my professional life I saw so many clients in a state of abject unhappiness, all of them vulnerable, sad and insecure, as were, probably, their spouses. Apart from the misery, all of them had one thing in common: they were in no emotional state to make life-changing decisions.

Emotions are feelings that come to us fully formed, that drive all human intercourse and influence all thoughts, but, and this is a huge but, they are things which we can neither comprehend nor control. To understand how complex the problem is, consider this. Dealing with divorce I discovered two paradoxes. The first is that when people are called upon to take important decisions, they are in no emotional state to do so. The second is that when people are unhappily married they become emotionally divorced, whereas when they are divorced a surprisingly large number feel emotionally married.

Such is the effect of emotions. And this fascinated me: at the very moment when people need their cool and sufficient detachment to make one of the biggest decisions of their lives, they succumb to their emotions. Their common sense and judgement desert them.

And so follows a bad divorce after a bad marriage. The marital knot is cut when, in wisdom, it could so easily have been untied.

These considerations prompted me to write a book on the emotional side of divorce. Entitled *If Divorce Is the Only Way* (1997, Penguin), it explains the advantages of pursuing a good divorce. Based on positive thinking with a reach target of moving on with minimum damage to the children and future relations between the parties, it has helped a lot of people.

To achieve this, my advice was to be aware of negative emotions and to get rid of them as quickly as possible, but I had no more understanding at that time of the nature of our emotions or how to handle them than anyone else. I pondered on this long and hard and began reading quite widely about emotions. I was particularly interested as my eldest child, Hugo, was about to become a teenager, something which as a young child he'd thought one had to take an exam to become! And this, and the desire to remain a few steps ahead of my son, brought me to a collaboration with a distinguished psychiatrist friend to write a book on adolescence. Every few weeks my friend would discuss a topic with me which I would then include in our next chapter.

Looking at Hugo, and indeed at his younger sisters and brother, childhood seemed such a carefree, happy time, yet everything was slated to change with the onset of adolescence. Suspended between childhood and adulthood, teenagers often become secretive, introverted, withdrawn and full of private fears. Previously ready smiles give way to sulky faces, relationships that had been trouble free become charged and confrontational, as the former loving and well-balanced child loses herself in a state of anguish and confusion.

Of course it's only a matter of time before things sort themselves out and balance is restored, but the few years of raging hormones and wild emotions when the adolescent is neither child nor adult certainly take their toll not just on the child but on her entire family. But again, the problem is emotions and when these are not understood by either child or parent a great deal of suffering can result.

And this is where I had my Eureka moment, for half way through the book I raised my sights to the adult world and realised there was a positive vacuum of understanding about the role that both emotions and love play in our lives. And this in turn led me to put aside the book on adolescence in favour of a far larger study of the human condition.

Such was the genesis of this book, which is about far more than emotions or, indeed, love, although you will see that everything ultimately revolves around their interaction.

All of us are human. Just as we all require sleep, we all share the same wants, needs and desires. But, sadly, we also all share the same ignorance of our true condition. It follows that to live life without understanding how we function must be the ultimate of follies.

But we no longer need to live like this, meekly accepting our ignorance as part of how life is meant to be. Because emphatically it is not.

Introduction

*'Humanity i love you because you are perpetually
putting the secret of life in your pants and forgetting
it's there and sitting down on it'*

E. E. CUMMINGS (1894–1962)

XLI poems (1925)

How can we function as sophisticated emotional beings when we can neither understand nor control our emotions?

That is the question.

This book is about nothing if not about being human. It is about love and human needs, about misunderstandings, tragedy, faith and despair, but mostly about love.

It is not another novel or self-help book, just a book that is truly stranger than fiction.

It is a book about us. It is a book of secrets, it is a book about life, about how life is protected and how it has been lived by a parade of humanity sixty five billion names long.

This book defines the human condition and the fundamental roles played in our existence by the greatest of all human needs,

1

the need to be loved. It translates the language and reveals the purpose of our emotions so that, at last, we can understand and take charge of them.

It discovers the secret of how life is protected, perpetuated and passed on. It introduces us to our all-important and previously unknown Supreme Sense, which will enable us to gauge how we are surviving at any one time and which is, crucially, the source of our self-awareness and consciousness.

It also introduces us to the concept of Nature's Morality and the promise of being able to enjoy all that we may have imagined for ourselves in the next world, in this one.

It holds out the beguiling prospect of our being able to resolve the majority of our emotional problems, in the future, with far greater facility.

Furthermore, in explaining the human condition, the book enables us to take charge of our emotions and our lives, providing us with the chance to feel, for the very first time, truly comfortable in ourselves and at ease in our nature.

I am a lawyer, not a scientist. However (a lawyer's word), this may have been an advantage in the long run as it enabled me to question things that experts appear to have accepted or, at least, never probed. I became intrigued by the notion that as the first and so far the only emotional beings we were, nevertheless, unable either to understand or to control our emotions.

For me, that single fact explained all human frailty. How could we be made so imperfectly? How could we be expected to control our lives if we could not control, let alone understand, our emotions?

Of course, we were not made so imperfectly and neither were we intended to live as victims of our emotions. It's just that no-one ever explained to us the human condition.

I started to read around the subject and three short statements stood out from all my reading. Put them together and you have the genesis of this book. I paraphrase them here:

> We are not at ease in our nature as are other creatures in theirs. (KAREN ARMSTRONG)
> We are unable to explain what it feels like to be alive (JACQUES BARZUN)
> Our emotions exist to save us from harm. (PETER WHYBROW)

These concepts are woven into the fabric, the DNA, of this book, one feeding off the other as conclusions begin to emerge. The result is here for you to read.

As human beings we have two special gifts from Nature not given so generously to the rest of Creation: our emotions and our capacity to love. To say that, between them, these two faculties explain everything is a gross over-simplification, but we will see that they stand at the very core of our survival. This makes our study all the more worthwhile, indeed almost tender, because whatever aspect of the human condition we consider, we are dealing with fallible, loveable, needy and vulnerable human beings, just like you and just like me. If we have been lost, we have all been lost together, as we are all irrevocably the same.

But then, as human beings, not only have we all gone wrong, historically we have never got it right. The following short anecdote makes the point well.

This is what happened one day in spring, when a Cro-Magnon caveman first invented the wheel.

It is one of those marvellous crisp days. Birdsong, blue skies, swelling buds, soon time to go elk hunting again.

The caveman has spent the long winter months chiselling and honing a slim rounded boulder until it is polished and smooth, perfectly formed and delightful to touch. With the coming of spring he pushes it home, surprised at how easily he manages to get it back to the cave.

He halts at the glowing embers of last night's fire, his excited voice rising to fill the cave entrance with sound. 'Come and see, you'll never guess what I've brought you!'

His wife emerges, an infant in her arms. Her pretty, vacant eyes stare at the stone now gloriously luminescent in the bright sun.

'Well, what d'you think?' the caveman asks proudly.

The wife moves the infant from one arm to the other, absent-mindedly shaking her head to flick a strand of hair from her eyes.

'What is it?'

The man is beaming now, chuckling to himself. 'Can't you see?' His large, callused hands stroke the wheel lovingly, then very gently he lowers it onto its side. 'It's a table!'

Our study is about the unique, unchallenged communion of humankind that turns out to be nothing more than a gross and terrible ignorance of the human condition, of how we function, of why we act and behave as we do and of how life would be better, far better, for everyone and all those yet to come, if only we could understand how things are meant to be.

It is as simple and as complicated as that. Going back through all the generations, through our parents and grandparents, and their parents and so on, right back to the first people to be recognisably the same as ourselves, everybody has got it wrong. In fact what was wrong was that when faced with a choice between two questions, everyone asked the wrong one. But that is the simple bit that comes at the end. The fact that our ignorance of the human condition is responsible for the vast majority of human problems, and much human misery besides, means that potentially nearly all such problems are solvable, enabling life to be immeasurably better, calmer, more rewarding and fulfilling.

The extraordinary thing that makes this book different from others is that all this is true. Can it be that complicated, can it be that simple?

In the Book of Ecclesiastes it is written: 'There is no new thing under the sun.' But there is. For we shall discover the key to all human understanding, not in the form of a belief or a concept or a theory, but in the form of a sense, our Supreme Sense, whose function and existence has passed humanity by, a sense that makes full sense of life. A sense, moreover, that makes full sense of love.

As in the opera which makes up our Prologue, God, Nature, Life, Humankind and Love, as the Five Pillars of Human Creation, influence and determine practically every aspect of our human existence, providing our architecture and infrastructure, defining us in every way, with the sole purpose of securing life's survival.

Life's survival, not our own. Paradoxical as it may seem, in the end life's entire purpose boils down to its own preservation. We, as human beings and bearers of life, are engineered to facilitate that. That is our sole function. But it has come at a very high price. How it affects us all is what we shall seek to explain.

For affect us it does. Every one of us, and indeed all those billions of individuals who have come before, have lived their lives with a comprehension of themselves and the way in which they function that is fundamentally wrong.

From that single mistaken belief has flowed the entire course of human dealings, from family and marital relationships, to love, religion and war, directly affecting the happiness and wellbeing of every person who has ever lived. Life could have been different, catastrophes and mistakes of history might have been avoided, things we would prefer not to have happened might not have done so, if only people had correctly grasped their own make-up.

This truth affects every single living human being. All of us are human and respond to what it means and feels to be human in exactly the same way, and, deep down, all of us know that we have yet to find the answers required to give meaning to life, to bring understanding to our existence, to find a better way of living.

Our opera is not just an amusement. Many of our problems are comprised in the tale that it tells, from our inability, as emotional beings, to control or understand our emotions, to our feeling ill at ease in our nature, to our failure to benefit from the virtues of love, all of which disable us from leading balanced lives. If this were not so, then ask yourself: why do a majority of people believe in an afterlife characterised by the absence of problems, which are the problems that they encounter in this life?

We shall carefully consider the Five Pillars of Human Creation, examining each of Life, Nature, Love, God and Humankind, and their inter-connection with each other. In this way we shall look at almost every aspect of what it means to be human, explaining the why and how of our make-up, dispelling our ignorance of the human condition and providing, through what I shall term, and later explain, Nature's Morality, a way of living a happier, more fulfilling life in a manner that provides in this world all the benefits expected in the next, with or without God.

As we proceed we shall encounter a riddle and a trick (yes, we have certainly been tricked) and a mystery, combining in true Churchillian fashion to present us with a 'mystery, inside a trick, wrapped in a riddle'. Any similarity to a 'riddle, wrapped in a mystery, inside an enigma' is inevitable, but Churchill employed his terms to describe his bafflement as to Soviet intentions before the Second World War, whereas we shall use ours to reveal the truth we are seeking, enabling us to explain emotions and love and to introduce the Supreme Sense and Nature's Morality.

Before we proceed a certain element is in need of clarification. If you are about to put away this book protesting that, although we shall never know the truth, God and Nature do not exist, or perhaps, as Spinoza believed, are one and the same, please consider this.

Strictly speaking, it is acknowledged, there is no such thing as Nature. Nature does not actually exist, but is merely the process of evolution, a process that, after its debut in Darwin's 'warm little pond' in the form of a single-celled organism, so tiny as to be invisible to the naked eye, took three and a half billion years to bring life to us. However, as everyone understands and uses the term and as the notion of Nature advances us on our journey by simplifying and humanising points to be developed, we shall continue to refer to Nature.

As for God, to some he too does not exist, because his existence is a matter of faith. But God will appear many times in these pages, for so absolutely is he enshrined in humankind that unthinking him is beyond our capacity to imagine. Having said that, however, you may regard him differently once you have read the two chapters devoted to him in this book.

Now, before we take a closer look at Life, let us consider what appears to be a simple, straightforward, and indeed, an essential question, which we alluded to a few pages ago: What does it feel like to be alive? All of us experience the feeling of being alive, every moment of every day, but, astonishing as it may seem, the likelihood of your getting the correct answer is very slim.

Think about it as you read on. You may consider it odd if we, who are alive, are unable to say what being alive feels like, but then, you will discover there is a very great deal about being human that we do not understand.

At some time or other, we have all seen the wheel and called it a table. And this is my point. We wouldn't drive a car, extract someone's appendix or fly a plane without knowing how, yet we live our lives in complete ignorance of how we are meant to function.

We were not provided with a manual when we came into this world but it is hoped that this book will be the next best thing. For this book explains the human condition. This is how it is.

Prologue

GÉRONTE: *It seems to me you are locating them wrongly, the heart is on the left and the liver is on the right.*
SGANARELLE: *Yes, in the old days that was so, but we have changed all that and now we practise medicine by a completely new method.*

MOLIÈRE (1622–73)
The Doctor in Spite of Himself (1925) Act 2, Scene 4

We are in an opera house packed to the rafters with an audience of the world's greatest and best, the richest and most famous, the most powerful and celebrated. Very few of them, despite their great distinction, are exempt from the general disappointments and emotional problems affecting most of humankind.

The lights have dimmed, so that before the curtain rises the golden tiers have relinquished their gleam, and the keen, intelligent faces glued to the stage have merged into a blank and characterless mass. All is still, anticipation palpable, when, taking everyone by surprise, a strange, powerful, quite unworldly sound, forlorn, plaintive and haunting, violently pierces the silence. It is too late for second thoughts now: the shrill sequence of discordant notes, blown with increasing volume through an ancient Hebrew *shofar*, a ram's horn, and solemnly repeated nine times, is summoning the people into the very presence of Almighty God.

Not even a first night for Mozart or Verdi, not even a first night for Mozart and Verdi, could have been like this. For this, the very grandest of grand operas, stars the greatest, most omniscient, sublime and powerful forces in all Creation, against which even a pope appears no more than a grasshopper.

Tonight, for one night only, the Five Pillars of Human Creation, without whom there would be no human existence, or existence of any kind, are about to perform.

Never before has there been such a production. But then, never before have God, Nature, Life, Humankind and Love condescended to appear together before humanity.

Based on the story of Life, Humankind and Love, the opera is a tale of misunderstanding, missed opportunity and dysfunction. You may even recognise it as our own tragic tale. Here is a brief synopsis.

Act 1
We see two impossibly beautiful women, a mother and daughter, Nature and Life. Life is her mother's adored child, the greatest, by far, of all her many treasures.

But there is a problem. Nature sings of her devotion to Life, lamenting that she created Life by accident, not knowing quite how she did it and not believing that she will ever be able to do it again.

Despite her exquisite beauty and sweetness, Life feels incomplete because she cannot exist alone. At once the source of all Creation, Life has still to depend upon Creation for her own existence. For she cannot survive without Creation, just as Creation cannot survive without Life.

Having to rely upon Creation to protect Life has therefore become Nature's abiding concern, causing her to engineer Creation especially to ensure that Life is effectively taken care of and protected whatever the cost. In this she succeeds, until Humankind evolves. The most advanced and adroit of all species, handsome and intelligent, yet, as Nature soon discovers, deeply flawed, Humankind becomes involved with Life, at first beguiling, then seducing and finally marrying her.

Nature comes to realise that the protections she has put in place for Life with the rest of Creation are not enough for Humankind. Humankind has a mind of his own and can, more or less, do as he likes. As he fails to care sufficiently for Life or to fulfil her needs Nature rapidly becomes anxious.

Act 2
The scene is thus set. As a mother, Nature is passionately all-caring, but as a mother-in-law she is cynical and suspicious and deeply mistrustful of Humankind's attitude to Life.

Fearful for her beloved Life, Nature secretly alters Humankind's make-up, equipping him with emotions she is confident will help him to look after her daughter.

But this only makes matters worse. Humankind's emotions absolutely overwhelm him. Unable either to understand or control his emotions, Humankind becomes confused, unhappy and uncomfortable. Indeed, he is no longer at ease in his own nature, as the rest of Creation are in theirs, and he remains no better disposed to the needs of Life.

Now desperate about what else she can do to induce Humankind to become more sensitive to Life's needs, Nature introduces him to Love, a benign and transient spirit well known for bringing people together. But this, too, has unforeseen consequences. Looking for comfort and support in his misery, Humankind readily turns to Love but instead of leading him back to Life, as Nature had planned, Love takes him to his long-estranged father.

Charismatic, all-powerful, all-controlling and jealous, Humankind's father is God, and God has waited a long time to receive his son. In a glorious reconciliation, representing one of the highlights of the opera, Humankind is united with his father, who demands and is given the very love, loyalty, devotion and trust that Nature had intended Humankind should bestow upon Life.

And so, increasingly neglectful of Life and forfeiting all chances of marital happiness in pursuit of his own, Humankind remains with God, never approaching his potential or perceiving his loss or the continuing hurt he has caused Life.

The opera concludes in a tumultuous quartet of the most profound sadness sung by God, in all his glory, Nature,

Life and Love, in an overwhelming climax regretting Humankind's wasted opportunities, his blindness to all that Life had to offer, and his folly in concentrating on his own selfish desires instead of the wellbeing of Life.

Before the end Humankind himself joins with the quartet, his fine tenor voice breaking with heartache and regret.

It is rumoured that, before the writing of this book is completed, a third act will be added to the opera, offering the chance to make sense of disappointed lives, giving explanation to all existence, providing an end to ignorance, bringing an understanding of life and human needs that humanity has always craved. If this is so, it will be included as an epilogue and the opera will have a positive and happy ending after all.

It is hoped that this will be the case, for when the curtain falls at the end of Act 2 there is mute silence. No-one stirs in the shocked stillness of the ornate auditorium. Soon, though, sobbing is heard and more sobbing. Humankind has wasted his life but in our ignorance, we too have done the same. We have missed the point, squandering our chances, overlooking our blessings and wasting our lives.

A tragic opera but the opera is a reprise of our own story. Whether we give love to God or not is beside the point. It is our story, as we shall see.

1

The Human Story

*'Ignorance and credulity have ever been companions
and have misled and enslaved mankind.'*

ERASMUS DARWIN (1731–1802)

Once upon a time, so long ago that it may have been upon the very first time, some 600,000 years or so before India collided with Asia to form the Himalayas, and the long tapered fingers of North and South America finally managed to touch, before there were any such things as heartache, heartbreak, sadness or disappointment, when ambition had yet to be invented and insecurity, anxiety and self-pity did not exist, where not a single being suspected the existence of a Creator nor had the slightest anticipation of a tomorrow, a branch in a shrinking, drought-ridden forest in Africa suddenly snapped and crashed to the ground, causing a large and hapless ape to fall out of a tree.

The loud report of the breaking branch, the scream of terror from the ape and the chilling thud as he hit the ground brought instant silence to the forest, abruptly halting the chatter of the other apes in the trees and the squawking of birds as they swooped low beneath the cloudless sky.

Was the ape dead? Did he stir? Was that a groan? His family rushed to him, cooing and wailing at the mound on the ground, prodding him, patting him, cajoling him, until to general astonishment, the tree-ape painfully rolled over onto his side, and, with desperate slowness, raised himself up onto all fours, collapsed and was then up again, managing for a fleeting moment even to take one hand off the ground.

Gradually, the noises of the forest resumed. Without a glance about him the battered tree-ape hobbled away, his mate and two offspring by his side, as if the breaking bough had signalled their expulsion from the colony of receding trees that had been their home whilst unremitting drought had turned forest into desert and food, once plentiful, had become scarce.

Like Moses, like Jesus, the tree-ape, if he was capable of thought, must have gone to his eventual death believing himself to have been a failure. But he was no such thing. He was an Abraham, a father to the future. For the descendants of the apes in the trees remain in the forest to this day, whereas the descendants of the one who fell out of the tree are reading this book. Over time future generations would stand upright and walk on two legs, leaving hands free to fashion tools, to carry things, to feed a mouth, caress a cheek, and, yes, to prepare for the emergence of humanity itself.

Four million, less about forty thousand, years later lived the caveman whom we have already met, unaware that he was the grandson times 160,000 (or 320,000 if we take primate generations to be half as long as a human generation) of the hairy, malodorous, ravenous, unprepossessing ancestor whose weight or sudden movement had caused the dying branch beneath him to break. Looking up at a moon that is almost full, can he, in his most reckless of dreams, imagine that one day his descendants will walk on that moon? Gazing at the heavens now cream with stars, can he ever comprehend that the life that animates him, the life-force he strives each day to preserve, has travelled as far to reach him as the distance between where he stands on a rocky hilltop and the furthest-flung of those stars twinkling above him? Looking down to the valley beneath him, still and sleeping in the moonlight, can his mind ever grasp the notion that one day, an Ice Age away, there will be towns and cities down there, roads, cars, power-lines and trains and aeroplanes, too, soaring like eagles across the sky, that he, the hunted as often as the hunter, will become ancestor to the absolute masters of the world, destined in time to invent the wheel (again), conceive of agriculture, construct cities, create civilisation and discover God?

To think these thoughts will take a leap of imagination far too great for our caveman, for whom imagination is still a new toy. For he stands only in the lobby of human existence, some 1,600 generations away from where we stand today.

But, despite the separation of generations, there are certain things that we share with him.

Firstly, there is our physical, mental and emotional make-up. This is identical in all respects to our own, to the extent that if it were possible to bring up his child as one of ours, it would be no different to any modern child, mastering every aspect of our way of life from city existence to baseball to computers.

Secondly, there is our ignorance of the human condition and, more specifically, the protections put in place by Nature to preserve the life within us. Such ignorance has served greatly to restrict our emotional development to the extent that in emotional terms we have barely progressed further than our caveman.

Fast forward 1,460 generations or so. It is as recently as 3,500 years ago, one thousandth of the time since the original spark of life made its appearance on earth. We are in the heat of the day, standing at the foot of Mount Sinai as the mountain quakes, the voice of the horn waxes louder and louder and over two million children of Israel huddle together in absolute terror. God's voice is thundering through the tumult.

God, the all-seeing, all-knowing, omnipresent First Pillar of all Creation, is pronouncing his laws, customs, traditions and precepts to regulate all human conduct and all aspects of human existence. The scope of his laws is massive, the detail spectacular, and yet, despite his obvious concern for human wellbeing, never once does he mention, never once does he even hint at, the parallel but more profound effect that Nature's protections will have on humanity and on our entire experience of living in this world.

'I am that I am,' he declares.

But we are as we are, which is to say, not as we ought to be. We are as we have always been and the point is that as of now, after 1,600 generations of being as we are, we still do not understand how we should be.

Of course, God is the ultimate I. But we too, and no-one else apart from God, are also, each and every one of us, an I. We feel as I, we live as I, we need, think, dream, love and *are* as I; indeed, being I distinguishes us from every other creature on the face of the earth.

But being I has never been easy. Because Life has taken us for a ride. Not just a ride in the literal sense, with life riding within us through time, animating Creation as it passes down the generations through countless host bodies, for that is what life does. No, Life has taken Humankind for a very different kind of ride, one that has been the cause of the majority of human problems, leaving far too many good, well-intentioned but less than happy individuals to experience their time in this world as disappointing, unsatisfactory and sad.

Nature has wired us with protections for the life that rides within us, the life that we bear, protections that are unique to us and not given to the rest of Creation. And neither God nor anyone else has ever explained them to us.

In the nineteenth-century context of a God-fearing world reared in the concept of rewards and punishments, Heaven and Hell, it took an agnostic, Robert Ingersoll, to observe: 'In nature there are neither rewards nor punishments – there are consequences.' Well, our ignorance of Nature's protections has certainly had a consequence. It has been a constant and irredeemable disaster for humanity.

Insecurity, confusion and conflict have possessed Humankind as if the generations who preceded us had condemned us to repeat and repeat all their follies, failures and mistakes. We just do not understand the human condition, each of us a bundle of desires, beliefs, drives, needs, wants, feelings and passions, wrapped up in our ignorance and packaged in someone else's genes; each of us, plus seven billion others, all suffering from the same lack of understanding and self-delusion.

Indeed, so entirely unaware are we of Nature's protections, and so deeply have they affected our lives, that we have never found out how life truly ought to be lived, nor how we ought to feel and function as emotional human beings. For the human story is the story of Life and Humankind's morbid fear of losing it. It is the story of how our ignorance of Nature's protections of Life has undermined Humankind's ability to live Life as it should be lived. It is the story of how Humankind has never discovered how to be fully human. The human story, the greatest, most wonderful story, where everyone is a hero just for being alive, is one that we do not begin to understand.

What is it that we do not understand?

We do not understand that after all the causes, bonds, religions, cults, tribes, beliefs and passions that have held humanity together and torn it savagely apart, after all the tenderness, concerns, relationships and love that have joined humanity as one and, as often as not, seen it fall to pieces, the art of living is ultimately dedicated to the art of staying alive; that Life's entire purpose boils down to its own preservation; that the need for Life to survive within us, the need for us to stay alive, shapes our infrastructure, architecture, instincts, desires, wants, needs, dreams, relationships and all that we think or do; that Nature, to whom Life's perpetuation is all that matters, who has no concern for us at all as individuals other than as bearers of Life, demands this, for Creation exists solely to support the Life that passes through it.

And more.

We bear Life and want to live it, yet we cannot explain what it feels like to be alive. We are the undisputed masters of the world, the most gifted and talented of all creatures, yet we are not at ease in our nature whilst the rest of Creation is comfortable in theirs. As the first, and so far the only, emotional beings, our emotions determine the daily intercourse of our existence and yet they are quite beyond our understanding and control.

Life (with a big 'L') comes to us with protections affecting life (with a small 'l') in every way imaginable. And so, when it comes to living, Life trumps life every time.

When more adults in the United States than comprise the entire population of France are diagnosed as suffering from mental illness, substance abuse or dependencies, we can see that humanity has major problems. Such problems persist even though we have created civilisation and found God. Looking at life as it is lived today, it is probably getting worse.

That many people are unhappy, insecure and self-obsessed, that relationship breakdowns are rampant, disappointment and jealousy the norm, and that people, including children, routinely suffer as part of their daily existence, are indications of how wrong we have gone. We have got things so wrong that living the human story as we do, not understanding so much of Life, has blotted out from our conception all notion of how we could and ought to be, as if being as we are is how it is meant to be.

'I am the Lord your God,' God thundered, giving us laws to live by and traditions to observe, but in all his concern to bind us to him in obedience and faith he never mentioned Nature's concern to preserve the life within us, controlling the way we are and how we function, which affects us even more absolutely than God's laws affect our conduct and our duty to him. Whether we are aware of it or not, such provision by Nature is a statement of how things are, of how things work, not for the wellbeing of Humankind, not even for the glory of God, but solely for the perpetuation and protection of Life.

God is faith, Nature is fact. For God, certainly every human being is a soul to be loved, some would say to be saved, but, for Nature, each being, including human beings, is at best a form of conveyance, a courier, a means of transport in which to bear Life on its way to Eternity. At its simplest, God cares for Creation whilst Nature cares for the life that animates it. Between them God and Nature cover every aspect of human existence. But whilst we can elect whether to obey God's laws or to ignore them, we are all bound to Nature's laws and protections, whether we like it or not.

The fact is that Nature's protections for Life actually work. How else could Life have reached us, having travelled through all its myriad incarnations for the last 3,500 million years?

We share with our animal ancestors basic needs to survive and to procreate as supplemented, where appropriate, by instincts. We fully understand such basic protections. They are not the problem. No, it is the extra protections given only to Humankind that concern us. Because our ignorance of these has caused all our troubles. We shall, therefore, be concentrating on our extra protections, and when I speak of 'Protections' I shall be referring to them.

The story of how Life has been protected within us is by no means a simple one. It is ingenious, it is complex, and yet, as we shall see, what it describes is ultimately so perfect and entirely all-embracing, that, once known, we shall never believe how Humankind failed to work it out.

But, very sadly, we *have* failed to work it out. We have failed dismally, our wretched inheritance from past generations dooming us to get everything wrong. Fallible, vulnerable, insecure, not terribly happy, and largely ignorant of the human condition, we have passionately striven for love and personal survival, driven by emotions we have never been able to understand.

Nature's Protections have rendered us human, elevating us far above the rest of Creation, but no-one has ever explained how our emotions, our capacity to love and our Supreme Sense were meant to work. And so, observing Life as we live it means observing lives that are physically secure but utterly fragile in emotional terms, lives that are slaves to misunderstanding and ignorance.

Is it any wonder it has proved impossible to get things right? But we shall try to do so. Ultimately, we shall see that, despite 1,600 generations of missed opportunity, Nature's Protections were always designed to provide the most balanced human existence, both to protect the Life within us and to enable us to thrive. We shall explain Nature's Protections in detail, observing how the Riddle, the Trick and the Mystery combine and fit together with Love to fashion the human condition. Understanding how this happens will enable us to unravel Nature's complexity.

Solving the Riddle will reveal the actual and unexpected purpose of our emotions, a vital component of the human condition, unknown and unsuspected until now, enabling us the better to handle our emotions and deal with the world at large. Exposing the Trick, which exploits our desire to love, will show how, despite our ostensible freewill, Nature has engineered us so that our behaviour tends to support her determination to protect the life within us. Explaining the Mystery will show how the Riddle and the Trick provide essential detail to our Supreme Sense, uniquely helping it to gauge our survival and, just as significantly, enabling us to act and feel as the self-aware, fully conscious, emotional beings that we are.

And, finally, looking at Love, we shall see how Nature relies on our capacity to love and our great need to be loved, to help us to protect each other and to find fulfilment through our Supreme Sense.

Understand these key elements in our make-up and we shall understand the human condition. Understand the human condition and we shall understand how we should be. Understand how we should be and we shall understand how life could be immeasurably better.

To do this we must take a more detailed look at how Nature sets the rules for our existence through her concern for the protection of Life.

2

An Inheritance
of Love

A million, million spermatozoa
All of them alive:
Out of their cataclysm but one poor Noah
Dare hope to survive,
And among that billion minus one
Might have chance to be
Shakespeare, another Newton, a new Donne –
But the one was me.

ALDOUS HUXLEY (1894–1963)

'Fifth Philosopher's Song' (1920)

Teenager to parents in the course of a row: I didn't ask to be born!

Parents to teenager: Well, as the odds against you even being conceived were almost 500 million to one, we weren't exactly expecting you either!

What is it that we demand of others, give away, withhold, ration, keep for ourselves, trade, barter, succumb to and resist? What is it that we want so strongly but cannot handle, our constant need for which, accompanying us as we enter this world and remaining with us until our very last breath, shapes our daily experience of life determining our character, personality, moods, temperament and, especially, happiness? What is it that once given will cause grief unless it is returned, that we uniquely have to help us to survive, that God himself demands of us?

It is what Nature has given to us alone in all Creation, the better to protect her precious Life, a feeling sublime and finely tuned that once exchanged will add an extra source of care, another set of eyes and ears and quick reactions to watch out for us and keep us safe. It is passion, it is rapture, fulfilment and security. It is pleasure, it is purpose and makes full sense of our existence. It is what all life passes by, the source of generations and the very reason for our being.

Yes, of course, it is Love, Nature's ultimate form of protection, our ultimate aid to survival.

But beware, love should come with a health warning. For, founded as it is on emotions we do not understand as part of the human condition where we have got everything wrong, Love can never be straightforward. Rarely does it end in people living happily ever after. Indeed, if there is one thing that the world will agree on as the most likely cause of confusion, misunderstanding, anger, infidelity, jealousy and deceit, it is love.

Oh, Life is a glorious cycle of song,
A medley of extemporanea;
And Love is a thing that can never go wrong;
And I am Marie of Roumania.
    DOROTHY PARKER (1893–1967), 'Comment' (1937)

Love in this part of the world is no sinecure.
    LORD BYRON (1788–1824), in a letter to John Murray from
Venice (1818)

Love iz like the measles; we kant have it bad but onst,
and the latter in life we hav it the tuffer it goes with us.
    JOSH BILLINGS (1818–85), *Wit and Humour* (1874)

Love is like any luxury. You have no right to it unless
you can afford it.
    ANTHONY TROLLOPE (1815–82), *The Way We Live Now* (1875)

Love is just a system for getting someone to call you
darling after sex.
    JULIAN BARNES (b. 1946), *Talking It Over* (1991)

Remember that Love is Nature's gift to us and it will be no
surprise that the pursuit of love is a passion, a game, in which
practically every individual in existence will participate, if
not on a daily basis, then at least at some stage in their lives.
Loving is a huge human need but, ahead of us again, Nature
has ordained that being loved is by far the greatest human need
of all. We never tire of trying to satisfy it.

But we are not given love for love's sake. Nature has
programmed us to need love for the better protection of

our genes. It is a universal need. Whether we be worthy or undeserving, everyone reading this book, every single person the world over, absolutely wants, absolutely needs, to be loved above all, in the same way that every human being has wanted to be loved since the beginning of human time.

Indeed, running like an invisible thread throughout all our experience and dealings, the need to be loved is the most powerful influence in all human contact, even though the wreckage of love is all around us. And there is nothing we can do about it. Feeling loved is all that we aspire to. It is a personal validation in any relationship. Making them feel loved is genuinely the thing of most value that one person may give to another. We feel protected by love as this is how Nature programmed us to feel. Proximate to survival, our feeling loved is a need fulfilled and an ideal state in which to sustain the protection of our genes.

When love goes wrong, when people do not feel themselves loved, the resultant feelings of sadness, emptiness, anger and despair are the most profound and immediate sources of unhappiness and misery, and these will not entirely dissipate until a new source of love is found.

Whilst history may well appear to be a litany of conflict, it is in fact a story of love. Witness the endless triumph of hope over experience. Witness the lust, inter-dependence and devotion of private lives; witness the agony of love lost or our wondering whether we are loved at all. And, of course, also remember that all new life is created by an act of making love.

But when did it all begin? We cannot know for sure although we can guess at it, for the capacity to love and the emotions with which to bestow and receive love mark the inexorable emergence of Humankind from the animal kingdom. Love and emotions are the hallmarks of humanity, the gifts of Nature, permanently separating us from the less endowed members of Creation.

From an early date our capacity to love and our accompanying emotions must certainly have served as an unseen force regulating our closest personal relations, binding parents to children, children to parents, parents to each other, family to family and friends to friends, as a bulwark of support in an uncivilised and very dangerous world. Such was always Nature's intention, for love has always been a basic source of protection extending between loved ones over and above the Protections we are concerned with, the Riddle, the Trick and the Mystery. But it must be remembered that all Nature's Protections, whether in the form of love, our emotions or our Supreme Sense, are concerned only with one thing. Not with the protection of us as individuals, but with the protection of our genes, with the life we bear within us.

So let us ask another question. When did the act of sexual intercourse, what is universally termed as making love, actually become associated with love? Originally, was it not just an instinctive, reproductive act that couples engaged in much as the rest of the animal kingdom had for hundreds of millions of years?

Humankind inherited the same instincts to reproduce as the rest of the animal kingdom. So, the answer must be that love came to characterise the act of sexual intercourse only once it was realised that such intercourse led to the birth of a child. For Love, as the agent of Nature, has no more obvious culmination than the making of a new life.

But how or why did it first dawn on our caveman that if he entered his woman, as he was wont to do when all was still in the comfort of his cave late into the night, she might produce a child some nine months later? How did he come to link his penetration to a subsequent birth when, if he ever gave the matter thought, the two events must have appeared entirely separate and unconnected?

Whenever it was, as was inevitable in the earliest times, our caveman would have achieved two firsts. One, being the first human able to decide to have a child rather than just proceeding to have one by instinctive desire and, two, being the first human to associate love with the act of sexual intercourse. Both are the most human of achievements.

We have heaped distinction on our caveman, first as the inventor of the wheel and now by adding love to sex. But even he could never have imagined that his child, perhaps the first to be conceived in love, would in fact have been conceived by a process involving the fertilisation of an egg; let alone that the egg, at only one quarter the size of the full stop at the end of this sentence, would be fertilised by a single microscopic sperm, one 88,000th its size.

Nothing has changed about conception since our caveman's time, but it is a hazardous process. To achieve fertilisation the successful sperm has first to participate in a mad, murderous dash amongst hordes of fellow sperm comfortably exceeding in number the entire population of the world prior to the time of Jesus, or, to put it another way, equal to the adult male population of modern India.

Billed as a 'race for life', this process of conception is, to the contrary, a race to the death. For there can be only one winner (and, possibly, none at all) and the chances of emerging as the winning sperm are statistically inferior to those of a random citizen being elected as president of the United States.

You will find no runners up, no second or third places, no silver or bronze medals. After all the pushing and shoving, the screaming and kicking, the cheating and scheming, every single one of up to 500 million sperm which fails to fertilise the egg will simply roll over and die.

This is how Nature has decreed life should be passed on. The race is a lottery, a game of pure chance. Every person alive, everyone who has ever lived or is yet to be born, comes, came or will come from a winning sperm, each one unique and capable of helping to create a human being. Had a different sperm prevailed and fertilised your mother's egg, a totally different human being would have come into the world instead of you.

But that is of no concern to Nature, who wants simply to propagate life and has no concern for those who bear it. This extraordinary over-provision of semen (for all animals who have it) is part of Nature's way of ensuring the perpetuation of Life, to which she is irrevocably committed. As we shall repeatedly see, Nature prefers to minimise risk and over-provision is the best way to reduce it. So it is that trees throw off thousands of seeds dressed up as helicopters, conkers, acorns, cones, nuts, fluff and fruit to improve the chances of new life taking root. Crops are the same, as is all vegetation, and once their beauty has passed even flowers are designed to transform into seed pods. Similarly, a human male will vastly over-produce semen to impregnate his female, whilst she will have been born with all the eggs she will need during her entire reproductive life.

Just look at what this means in human terms. In the whole world, in any period of twenty four hours, an astounding 100 million billion sperm (100 followed by fifteen noughts), each one entirely individual and capable of fertilising a female egg to create a totally unique human being, will have arisen for selection to life. From out of these, a possible 250 million human beings might have been conceived, although the annual number of births in this world (after sixty million or so abortions) is about ninety million.

How so? Because, despite the violence, cruelty, danger and chaos of our times, the wars, bombings, rapes and murders, it is estimated that in every twenty four hours across the globe there are 250 million acts of sexual intercourse, possibly exceeding all the acts of violence by a margin. Apply an average sperm count of 400 million and multiply that by 250 million and you reach the figure of 100 million billion sperm in every period of twenty-four hours, every day of every week, year in, year out. In a relatively short period of time this will produce more potential candidates for election to Life than there are stars in the heavens or galaxies to contain them.

And Nature is up there with the stars as well. The light

from the stars we can see has taken years to reach us. Some stars are so far away that when the image we see of them was new, the earth, which is 4.6 billion years old, did not even exist. It follows that anyone then looking at our world from such a star would have seen nothing.

Stars are visible to the naked eye and yet we cannot see an individual sperm or a human egg, nor any of the trillions of cells that make up our bodies, without the aid of a microscope.

Just as every human being is ultimately descended from the same being, every one of our trillions of cells is descended from the same single fertilised egg. Each cell contains our own individual history and recipe for making us. Unravel our DNA from those cells and lay it end to end and you can encircle the earth 150,000 times – or, to put it another way, enough miles to set you well on your way to the nearest star.

But space travel, covering thousands and millions of years at the speed of light (186,000 miles per second) can never be a serious possibility for us whose ultimate limitation is our own mortality. A single lifetime is all we have, and even if we spent the bulk of it speeding through space, we would hardly have left the suburbs of our planet before our time was up. To reach the stars would require a way of cheating death. Most people who believe in immortality see it as a form of afterlife beginning when our lives are over, which, when you think about it, would leapfrog us from earth to eternity whilst Life labours on her way transferring from one body to the next.

To extend our experience of Life by thousands and millions of years would involve finding a form of living on, beyond our limited span. This could never happen unless a means were found for us to inhabit another's body, transferring as necessary from one body to another with each successive generation. Perhaps, then, eventually, we might reach the stars.

Unimaginable? Undesirable? Impossible? Of course it could never happen. But this is *exactly* what Nature provided for our genes, enabling Life to journey through the generations with genes spending merely the tiniest fraction of their existence in one human being before joining another. In fact this is exactly how Life has journeyed to reach us through time for three and a half billion years, since the original single-celled organism appeared in the primordial soup.

In this way, starting in the mists of time, our genes have travelled down the generations through parent and child for thousands of millions of years. Their messages, all but immortal, have brought Life to every human being whilst their continuing existence has depended upon their being passed on through offspring.

Set against the ages over which our genes have been travelling, our lifespan is nothing in the timescale of our genes. And so, as we would race to reach the stars, our genes ride within us, sheltered by our body, onward and onward from a past we never knew to a future we shall never see. Whilst they ride with us, they are our genes, duly protected by our personal capacity to love and our individual emotions.

But how does this work?

'Waiter, waiter, there's a single-celled organism in the primordial soup!'

'That's alright, Sir, it is the very spark of Life!'

'But, my good man, it's replicating before my very eyes!'

'Well, that's 'eredity, innit.'

If you have ever wondered why humans beget humans rather than rabbits, and lions give birth to lions rather than to leopards, it is because of heredity, a process of replication of like for like.

Heredity need never have happened, but it did happen once, 3,500 million years ago in Darwin's 'warm little pond', although it could just have easily have been a puddle, 'with all sorts of ammonia and phosphose salts, light, heat, elements etc.'. Unwitnessed, unwitnessable, it was a wondrous event marking the beginning of life and evolution in a glorious self-sustaining and ever-continuing burst of creation that goes on to this day and is likely to continue forever.

Another creation of Nature, heredity is the reason we are here, the process by which we arrived, the very passage of Life itself, as dressed, packaged and preserved in countless millions of previous incarnations, Life has travelled through 3,500 million years and billions of different hosts to reach us, so that we may first be made alive and, in living, pass Life on.

And that, from Nature's point of view, is all that matters. To us, life is the period between birth and death, but to Nature, notwithstanding all the immediacy of our lives, our lifetimes are merely stepping stones in Life's seemingly endless journey to eternity. We can chart that journey, imagining the stepping stones threading their way towards us until they become so close that we actually recognise them in the lives of our grandparents and parents.

In no study is this better achieved than in Richard Dawkins's quite remarkable book *The Ancestor's Tale: A Pilgrimage to the Dawn of Life*. As the title suggests, it guides us, in meticulous detail, all the way back through our ancestors to the beginning of life.

For our purposes, to see the progression of Life we need only to trace our ancestry back in time in broad outline. We do so via our parents and human ancestors and then, greatly abridging Dawkins's list, back to the apes and monkeys, lemurs, tree-shrews, rodents, marsupials, amphibians, lungfish, sharks, sea-squirts, protosomes, sponges, fungi and plants from which humankind is descended.

Of course, there would have been no stepping stones if our ancestors had not been survivors, surviving, that is, long enough to have offspring. For, by definition, each ancestor becomes a stepping stone for Life, enabling Life to continue on its journey for a single generation and so on through successive ancestors right down to ourselves. And we also bear Life and will become ancestors and stepping stones in turn, as we pass life onto our children.

As we shall continually have cause to observe, it is apparent that the essence of life is survival; that is the survival of the being, creature or thing that bears it for all too brief a period of time. Life depends on that survival for its continued existence, and it follows, quite marvellously and fantastically, that we are here today, not just because our human ancestors were survivors, but also because our pre-human ancestors were survivors as well, having survived for sufficiently long to replicate, as did their offspring in turn, in an unbroken chain down to ourselves.

It is surely right that if prior to bearing offspring our ancestor lungfish had been eaten by a squid, or our ancestor rodent had been flattened by a falling tree, or our ancestor lemur had eaten poisoned berries, we would not have been born. That is a fabulous thought that will be new to many.

All creation is united by the bearing of Life and also, having evolved from the same original organism, by an identical basic chemistry and genetic code. And so, a bat's wing, a dolphin's flipper and Daniel Barenboim's conducting arm all share an identical pattern of bone structure showing a common descent from a single ancestor. Our brains too have evolved in the same manner, ratcheting up from cobra, to rat, to a brain fit for Einstein by way of additions and refinements to a basic design.

And so, Life abounds, Life teems, Life thrives across the globe, on land, in oceans, in the air, in every living creature, in every plant and tree, within ourselves and about our persons. Life is everywhere, it is part of us, it happens. We can watch it happen, following in a matter of months as a fertilised egg forms into a breathing, feeling human being. We can watch as it stops happening when a being ceases to exist and becomes a lump of matter.

We are infused with Life, we are full of it, and yet we have no more idea than had our caveman of how or why a life-bearing human being should be created by the coupling of a single egg with a single sperm, of what Life is or where it comes from, or where it will go to when it leaves us. Once created, that Life is carried by our genes, which build our body in which that Life will survive. Such is Life. That's all we know.

3

Who Am I?

'*Who is it that can tell me who I am?*'
WILLIAM SHAKESPEARE (1564–1616)
King Lear (c. 1606), Act 1, Scene 4

A man drives into the wilderness. The tracks run out and he abandons his car, striding on through the scrub and into the desert. Hours later, coated in dirt, drenched in sweat, parched and exhausted, he finally stumbles, collapsing to his knees before a rocky promontory stained pink in the evening sun.

'Who am I?' the man pleads, his eyes shut so tight that it hurts, his very soul concentrating on this, his ultimate question as he faces up to the heavens.

Silence ensues. He waits. Seconds tick by, but nothing. He is about to give in to despair when a deep, velvety voice, booms from the sky.

'Who wants to know?'

Who are we?

Consider this. Imagine life without all that we take for granted. Not blaming our misfortunes on the weather, politicians or bankers. Not even electricity, the internet, money, affluence, success. No, more seriously, an existence without smiles, without laughter, without even tears.

Imagine a life where there is neither language nor choice of reaction, nor even the familiar dexterity of fingers and thumb.

Imagine actually living without self-recognition, without consciousness, a life totally bereft of all that makes us human: love, imagination, reason, emotions, hope.

Could any prospect be more desolate, more truly tragic and depressing? But what are we describing? Surely nothing less than someone cruelly reduced to little more than a vegetable?

Not at all. Tennyson's swallows may dip their wings in tears, but they cannot cry; a snail may lie contentedly upon a sun-drenched rock, but it cannot smile; young rabbits may play together in the morning sun, but they cannot laugh.

We're describing no more than animal life: how it is and how it has always been to be an animal. This is how Creation existed prior to humankind, and how the majority of Creation still does, responding to the great needs of survival and procreation whilst driven by an unchanging system of instinct and sensation unaware of God or interest rates, of Facebook or the price of gas.

Animals are what they are. A sheep is a sheep, a sparrow is a sparrow, a herring is a herring with no thoughts of improvement or change. Indeed, except through the long lens of evolution, progress is denied to them. As far as we know, most animals live without expectation, disappointment, pretension or ambition and they are comfortable living in this way. Each day is much the same as the last, the point of their existence being merely to get and beget, to live long enough to pass their genes onto offspring, and this seems to suit all animals, apparently comfortable in their limitations.

Subject to the cruel perils of survival of the fittest, this is how animals survive, and, more to the point, this is how Life survives within them.

Who are we? We are the only beings capable of understanding that question. We are not the same as other animals. With humankind it is different. Although we are descended from animals we are no longer the same as them. What we have that animals do not have is what makes us different and makes us human. And, despite the same Life pulsating within us, it is those differences that make us uncomfortable in being human, unable to understand ourselves, let alone who we are.

We can blame it all on Nature. It is Nature's Protections that make us so different to the rest of Creation. Nature's Protections have been both our blessing and our curse. That this is so is due not just to the massive size of our brains or our huge range of emotions, marking our superiority to the rest of Creation, but to a single extraordinary factor: that for all our brilliance and achievements, our ability to communicate, think, plan, remember and love, we can neither understand nor control our emotions. Our astute minds may be a battlefield where reason and emotions do combat, but we are the losers whichever one wins, for we have no idea how to handle our emotions.

It gets worse. Just as animals live and function without concept of self-recognition, so we live and function with emotions that present themselves already formed and hit us straight between the eyes, and we do not know where they have come from nor what they are really for.

And this has major consequences. For we, the masters of the world, are each of us obliged to conduct our lives subject to some inner force entirely beyond our control that seems to have taken us over as it challenges our judgement, determining how we feel and behave. But this is how emotions work. This is why, in our profound ignorance, so many of us live unsatisfactory, frustrated lives. Such is the way life is and has always been. Indeed, such is the true cost of our ignorance.

That such an essential, fundamentally important component of our being, affecting every aspect of our daily existence, should be beyond our understanding and outside our control, is an astonishing thought. That we should always have lived this way, the victims of emotions and passions that we cannot master, is beyond belief. As emotional beings, not to understand or control our emotions means not being able to control or understand ourselves. Is it unsurprising, therefore, that founded on our emotions, love does not always work?

We have reached the fault line in the human condition. Consider what this means. There is not a single thought, action, feeling, prayer, barely a sensation, that is without emotions. Emotions are the currency of all human dealings and experience, but, extraordinary as it may seem, whilst they speak with our voice, emotions communicate in a language that we simply do not comprehend.

In the pages that follow we shall learn how to understand that language; indeed all will be explained, as we meet the Riddle, the Trick, the Mystery and ultimately our Supreme Sense.

But there is an obstacle in our path which we must clear before we make real progress. A barrier to further insight which we have to overcome. It constitutes a stop on further understanding, explaining why we and previous generations have remained ignorant of the human condition.

However, enough words.

To specifics.

Tucked away in the text of *The House of Intellect*, a celebrated book by French-American educator Jacques Barzun, that has absolutely nothing to do with our subject, is a single sentence at once so intriguing and sublime that it could form a course of study on its own.

> If it were possible to talk to the unborn, one could never explain to them how it feels to be alive, for life is washed by the Speechless Real.

Well, what does it feel like to be alive?

That, of course, is the question I raised in the Introduction. The notion that we are unable to explain that feeling is very strange when each of us, in a world population of seven billion, experiences those very feelings every second of every day.

So, what is the problem? Let us go back to Barzun. If it were possible to pursue the beguiling concept of talking to the unborn – who, of course, have no idea what it feels like to be alive – how would we explain that feeling of being alive, at once so familiar to us, yet apparently beyond our capacity to describe, a feeling, moreover, that is identical to all humanity?

Well, how does it feel to be alive? How does it feel to you, now, at this very moment before your eye reaches the question mark at the end of the sentence?

People's experiences of life are necessarily individual, unique, separate and different, but when it comes to feeling alive, that seemingly indefinable sensation is exactly the same for everyone. We can describe both our huge lexicon of emotions, familiar feelings of anger, jealousy, gratitude, happiness, sadness, of being insecure, unloved, distressed, ecstatic, awestruck, contented, joyful. We can describe the physical sensations of being alive, our senses of seeing, hearing, thinking, tasting, touching and pain. We can describe the thoughts we have, the dreams, resentments, hopes and plans, the relationships we belong to, the needs, desires, wants of being human, affecting all that we do. Each feeling, each experience, each sensation may be individually described but, unlikely as it may seem, we have no words to explain the actual feeling of being alive.

Who are we? How can we begin to answer without being able to state what the feeling comprises?

It is not just a question of vocabulary. We are looking for something that necessarily embraces every possibility of sensation and expression, every single permutation of the human condition, as shared with seven billion separate individuals alive at this time, each a solitary being experiencing every sensation as a unique entity, as the only person able to think his or her thoughts, to feel his or her feelings and to sustain his or her wellbeing.

Our problem is massive. How could anyone perm a constant feeling of being alive from such an infinite and ever-changing equation? What does it feel like to be self-aware, the individuals we are, the private persons we know we are, the inhabitants of our bodies, the directors of our brains, the thinkers of our thoughts, the dreamers of our dreams, multiplied by seven billion?

So, how do we do it? We must look within ourselves and see if we can find a constant present in all human experience, something we may have overlooked or never appreciated that we had.

To do this, we must attempt the impossible. We must try to synthesise all the passions, feelings, thoughts, prayers and beliefs, all the moods, reactions and emotions which, together, make up the human experience of being alive, and see if we can extract from that a single factor that is present in them all. It is like seeking an alchemy, reducing all experience to a feeling we can describe; it is like discovering the Philosopher's Stone.

The term 'Speechless Real' is apt to describe the apparent impossibility of this task. Life, as we live it, is not, and never has been, that simple. Washed by the Speechless Real, our lives make insufficient sense to us. Our emotions, our personal responses to all experience are beyond our understanding and control. We function. We exist. But we drown in the Speechless Real with needs we do not realise we have, senses we do not recognise and powers we do not see.

For, travelling through the generations just like Life itself, the Speechless Real engulfs us in a wave of confusion, placing scales upon our eyes so that our frailties, inadequacies, excesses, limitations, even our inhumanities, which render us inferior to lesser species, become the reality of living. All life is indeed washed by the Speechless Real so that we are not aware of its limitations. We do not know that there is anything more to life and living than the way we see it, that there is anything wrong with the way we live, that there may be a better way of living, that we have never even approached our potential.

The Speechless Real envelops us all. Unspoken, tacit, yet as immutable as the bones we are fashioned with, it is a blight upon all human existence.

We seem to be faced with an insurmountable problem over something so obvious, as how to describe the feeling of being alive. But, of course, it can be done and we shall do it. Indeed that very feeling will be defined when we discover our Supreme Sense.

But, deep within our problem lies a tremendous irony. All of our difficulties of definition, lack of ease, human frailty, of not functioning as we are meant to, have arisen because of the manner in which Nature has protected the Life within us. And this, in turn, has given rise to an almost universal departure from fact and logic, to support a fantasy, a fiction, a romance, a fancy, a conjecture, a vision, a caprice, yet an article of the profoundest conviction and faith, embraced still and passionately believed in by a majority of humanity.

The belief in a next world to right the wrongs, assuage the hurts, reward the virtues, and punish the sins of this world is part of most religions and of folklore in practically every culture. It is the ultimate promise of peace, of bliss, of reunion, the end of earthly troubles, an infinite time of grace and harmony, of rest and comfort.

There are as many visions of the next world as there are people who conceive of an afterlife. It is the stuff of imaginings and dreams, of faith not fact. Of faith in gods, in God, in fate, in wishful thinking, in the need for there to be more to our lives than the brief and often unhappy years spent on earth, in the desire to reduce the pain of grief when a loved one dies, in the belief that we shall see them again.

The notion of an existence hereafter is the consequence of the shortcomings of this world. Our ignorance of the Protections of Life has caused insurmountable problems and endemic distress. And so, commencing as our bodies lie rotting or burnt, after Life has left us, immortality will again provide Life to us, or to our soul or spirit, which we never encountered in life, in the realm of Heaven.

Whether this is practicable, and if so how, is not for us to say, but what seems certain is that the concept of the next world essentially envisages the shedding of all we found burdensome in life in favour of a new existence where human unease and human distress and human strife are completely banished. All is fulfilment and, after our all too brief and miserable lives, all will be wholesome, troubles will be shelved and joy will reign for all eternity.

In short, what the concept comes down to is that our earthly troubles and the things we do not like in this world will be left behind and forgotten. And all those troubles and all that we do not like in this world have come about due to our inability to recognise and understand the protections in place for the Life within us and our consequent unease at being as we are.

We yearn for such an existence because we seek a greater purpose that is more than suffering. At all costs we wish to avoid Joseph Addison's 'secret dread, and inward horror, of falling into nought'. But then, we must also remember the words of H. L. Mencken: 'The most costly of follies is to believe passionately in the palpably not true. It is the chief occupation of mankind.'

It appears that, as a result of our ignorance, Life has been protected at the cost of human wellbeing. Our shared ignorance, frailties and inadequacies are an accepted part of what we are, as much a cover for the human condition as the clothes that we wear. If we can grasp this and remove from our eyes the scales of the Speechless Real, then a stunning prospect awaits us.

There exists the possibility that, with or without a belief in God, we could have all the benefits of the next world in this one. That this is so is a major premise of this book. I shall explain how it can so easily come to pass in the chapters that follow.

Who are we? Who wants to know?

4

A Little Magic

Pooh began to feel a little more comfortable, because
when you are a Bear of Very little Brain, and you
Think of Things, you find sometimes that a Thing
which seemed very Thingish inside you is quite different
when it gets into the open and has people looking at it.

A. A. MILNE (1882–1956)
The House at Pooh Corner (1928)

There can have been no rustling leaves, no mottled sunlight, for there were no trees, no vegetation of any kind on that unique day (or was it night?) that Life made its first appearance on earth some 3,500 million years ago. But let us hope that it was daytime and that rain, merciful, generous rain, was falling from a sunny sky, for there should have been a rainbow to mark the birth of Life.

Rainbows are made up of raindrops adorned in all the colours of the spectrum through refracting light. Looking at a rainbow it is hard to imagine that what we are really observing is an arc of falling rain. What we see we assume to be real, but the rainbow is comprised of millions upon millions of separate raindrops silently falling to earth.

When we behold a rainbow we see its colours, not the individual raindrops from which it is formed.

And this is the point. When Nature beholds Creation and the beings that comprise it, she sees not the countless billions of individual creations that bear Life. She sees only the Life that animates all Creation.

We have a difficulty. The Speechless Real has not only prevented us from understanding the human condition, it has also prevented us from realising that we do not understand it. And so, we live, as all previous generations have lived, difficult, sometimes disappointing lives, often in a state of distress, anxiety and misery, unaware of why our lives are like this or of how, if we only understood the human condition, Life could provide us with a better and more fulfilling existence.

As Jacques Barzun observed, the Speechless Real has prevented us from being able to explain what it feels like to be alive, so our solution must lie in finding the words denied to us. This observation by Max Planck compounds our problem: 'Science cannot solve the ultimate mystery of nature. And that is because, in the last analysis, we ourselves are part of nature and therefore part of the mystery we are trying to solve.'

So does this mean that we, as part of the mystery, have reached an impasse, gone as far as we can go? Indeed, where can we possibly travel from here to solve a mystery of which we form a significant part?

Like Planck, Barzun made it clear that the answer we are seeking cannot be found from our own cerebration. Simply being alive disqualifies us from access to the very knowledge we are searching for. What can we do? Can there be anyone whose life is not washed by the Speechless Real? Is there someone somewhere, perhaps, who can see what we cannot see, and explain what no-one has ever explained in more than forty thousand years?

We need to find a pair of innocent eyes, a witness to the way we live. Someone who could look at us untrammelled by the Speechless Real, and, having observed us, provide the words we are seeking to describe the feeling of being alive.

But how? Who?

This will not be the first time that a book summons up a little magic to solve a problem. Therefore, as we have nothing to lose but our ignorance, please excuse me if I introduce some magic now to help us overcome this very real problem.

As an almost-person still of minus years, human though not yet human at all, the Unborn Child may be born tomorrow, but he is not a full-blown human being today. And so, today, he is not yet part of the problem, not yet ensnared by the Speechless Real.

I therefore propose standing Barzun's premise on its head. Instead of trying to provide explanations to the Unborn Child, I intend asking him to provide explanations to us.

This is where the magic comes in, along with your indulgence, as I propose investing him with the power of perception, the sagacity and faculties of a great US president, of, say, a Washington, Jefferson, Lincoln or FDR, to give sense and value to his observations. He can then see what we cannot see, understand what we fail to understand, glimpse a view of Life and hold it for as long as it takes to explain it to us, a glimpse uncorrupted by our confusion, unblemished by the Speechless Real and, being beyond the scope of Planck's observation, free of all our collective emotional baggage and inertia, erroneously accepted as part of human nature for the last forty thousand years.

Perhaps he could then discover why, search as we may for the happiness, love, security and meaning that all the hearts of Humankind so keenly desire, we seldom find the things we are most urgently seeking. Perhaps he could explain what no human being has ever been able to explain, enabling us to break the shackles of our ignorance that have emasculated all Humankind.

We live in a fog of confusion, never far from the brightest light yet never close enough to see it. We cannot solve the problem by ourselves. So let us produce the Unborn Child. Let us provision him with genius, all our hopes, and sufficient magic, and hear what he has to tell us, which no other human being will have heard before. Unconventional our path may be, but a great deal is about to be revealed.

And so, to the Unborn Child. The still, small voice of the president yet to come, his sweet, delicate face a study of innocence, a study of beauty, is about to speak.

UNBORN CHILD: Life did not begin and does not end with human beings. The only purpose of existence is to convey Life in an extraordinary relay through time. You may feel as if the laws of Nature do not apply to you, but they do.

51

You are the first, and so far the only, emotional beings. Your emotions constitute the very essence of your being human, and yet you live your lives and bring up your children unable to either understand or control your emotions.

If, as emotional beings, you can neither understand nor control your emotions, the very characteristics that make you into emotional beings, there must be something that you are doing wrong or have misunderstood or overlooked, for Nature does not fashion imperfections.

Reflect for a moment. You would never try to fly a plane, to defuse a bomb, conduct surgery, even to drive a car, or speak a foreign language, without first understanding how it was to be done. And yet you, and all those who came before you, have not had the slightest qualms in leading your lives and ordering the lives of others, quite unable to understand or, indeed, to control the very things that enable you to live and function. Instead you live your lives as victims of your emotions rather than as their masters, with disastrous consequences.

'A little neglect may breed mischief; for want of a nail the shoe was lost, for want of a shoe the horse was lost, and for want of a horse the rider was lost.' And so it is with human ignorance. By not understanding the human condition other great truths are also lost.

AUTHOR: That's Benjamin Franklin, isn't it? One of the great American Founding Fathers? Goodness, you've certainly acquired—

UNBORN CHILD: Please! Of course, you didn't come into this world with a manual explaining how to live your life. Instead, you and all of Humankind have relied upon your parents and family, your teachers, philosophers, sages, friends and priests, to show you how life should be lived. But all of them, going back to the first Cro-Magnon men and women, have got it spectacularly wrong.

AUTHOR: Wrong? Heavens. How's it been wrong? How...?

UNBORN CHILD: I am your witness, but I do not have much time to explain. I am shortly to be born. I am about to live. When I am born a single gasp of air will join me to the living and I shall carry Life, bear it and protect it until the day Life leaves me and I die. I will have exchanged the certainty and comfort that is the womb for a predominant state of ignorance, misunderstanding and uncertainty, casting everyday existence into great confusion.

I am witness to the primal pleasures of human existence, to the human condition whose brain and emotions raise Humankind far above all other beings. I am witness to the depth and range of human feelings denied to the rest of Creation. I am witness to good people finding life a disappointment, to things going wrong and life not turning out as it should. I am witness, too, to soaring spirits and great hope.

I am witness to all these things, to how the characteristics of the human condition are bound together in a manner, and for a purpose, that Humankind has yet to understand.

AUTHOR: But... No, please go on.

UNBORN CHILD: As your witness I can see Life as you cannot see it. I can see Life as it is, Nature's most treasured creation passing down the generations on its journey to eternity. I can see humanity's mistake, for you do not understand how Nature has seen fit to protect Life within all human beings. I can see Humankind's error in believing only in the overriding importance of individual lives, when Nature is concerned not with the individuals who bear Life but the safe passage of the Life that they bear.

This thought is the key to understanding human problems. Nature's concern for you is limited to protecting and perpetuating the Life within you. The way that Nature achieves this, to provide for your survival as host bodies to Life, explains the human condition. Because Life did not begin with human beings. It has existed for billions of years. It is borne by every living creature, every living thing, and, despite all belief to the contrary, the true and sole purpose of all existence is to convey Life to the next generation, in an extraordinary relay through time. For you are not just some form of survival machine, you are first and foremost bearers of Life.

AUTHOR: Bearers of Life. But surely Richard Daw—

UNBORN CHILD: My time is short. Allow me to continue. I understand what is happening to me every day as I continue to develop in utero. How does this happen? Through my genes. Genes are the linchpin of all existence but also the means by which Nature provides for the perpetuation of Life. In your opera, genes are how Nature engineers Creation for the protection of her daughter. For genes bring Creation to Life as surely as they bring Life to Creation. As Nature's instrument in preserving Life, genes are the architects, engineers and builders of us all, constructing and wiring Creation appropriately so that we may become the beings we are supposed to be.

Without genes there would be no human or any kind of beings, no trees or any kind of vegetation, no life, in fact, no Creation of any kind. It follows, therefore, that being concerned, above all, to perpetuate Life, Nature's overwhelming priority must be to protect our genes.

Consider genes from Nature's viewpoint. Integral to all creation, they are faithful to Nature in all respects, serving, as they do, Nature's determination to perpetuate Life.

AUTHOR: Faithful? Not selfish? Surely, I thought, Rich—

UNBORN CHILD: Selfish? Why selfish? This is why genes exist. They feel nothing, care for nothing and intend nothing save for their own survival. Far from being a selfish desire, that concern to survive is essential to fulfil Nature's purpose, enabling Life to continue on its journey through successive generations of host bodies. In other words, genes have no alternative but to be faithful to Nature and her schemes for Creation. If they were not faithful, Life would simply come to an end.

AUTHOR: Oh, I see.

UNBORN CHILD: We come now to a very significant juncture. How does Nature protect our all-important genes? As I am not yet going anywhere on my own, my genes are protected by my mother. But how are her genes protected and those of every other human being? Having regard to Humankind's volatile nature, imagination and freewill, Nature is not minded to rely solely on the safeguards she has provided for the rest of Creation. How many people would you trust with your life twenty four hours a day, every day?

Nature does not take chances. With other animals, Nature has provided primary needs to survive and procreate, thereby protecting both the genes and their hosts. She has endowed Humankind with the same great needs and the sensations and instincts that crucially support them, but she has also given Humankind something more.

What is it that Humankind has that is not given to other animals, something exclusive to you as emotional beings that mark you out from the rest of Creation? Well, if you're not conscious of providing protection to your genes, it must be something over which you have no control.

Can you guess where this is heading?

AUTHOR: I'm not sure. Our...? No, please go on.

UNBORN CHILD: Nature gave you your emotions to protect your genes.

AUTHOR: Our emotions?!

UNBORN CHILD: If genes had faculties like Humankind, emotions would be their eyes and ears. As long as Humankind survives, your genes will survive, but they will do so because your emotions protect them.

AUTHOR: But all our happiness depends upon our emotions, our welfare, sense of wellbeing, our moods, temperament, passions. We have emotional personalities, our lives depend upon our emotions for fulfilment, we have no lives without them. So how can it possibly make sense to say that our emotions serve the interest of our genes rather than ourselves?

UNBORN CHILD: I'll tell you. Evolving as bodily functions such as fight-or-flight responses, emotions originally served to protect your genes by helping to keep your ancestors alive and procreating in a very dangerous world. Those responses are instinctual. Today, for conscious beings, emotions serve exactly the same purpose.

As protectors of your genes, your emotions react to all of your experiences, responding negatively when there is a perceived threat to the fundamental need to survive, and positively when attaching themselves to your genes' need to procreate, or just love.

In this way, you respond to danger, threats, hostility and harm with anger, fear, aggression, defiance, hate and other gradations of negative emotions. On the other hand, you respond to help, love, charity and kindness with gratitude, appreciation, affection, love and kindness yourselves.

Whilst there are twice as many negative emotions as positive ones, the inescapable fact is that all of them present themselves complete and various and quite beyond any control. This is because they are responding to the needs of your genes rather than to your personal interests as you would perceive them. Not only do you not control your emotions, it appears that it is your emotions that control you, causing you to behave in the way you do in order to protect your genes.

AUTHOR: So, somehow in this way, emotions save us from harm?

UNBORN CHILD: Exactly.

AUTHOR: So, let me just check this out. Whilst there is little risk of confronting a tiger as we walk up Sloane Street to Knightsbridge, causing our fear responses to kick into action, we can still find ourselves pushed off the pavement outside Harvey Nichols, caught by the rain without an umbrella, stood up for lunch, perhaps mugged, sacked from our job, or dumped by a girlfriend's text. Presumably all of these things would excite our negative emotions as if our survival, and that means our gene survival too, were under threat?

UNBORN CHILD: Exactly.

AUTHOR: Or, on the other hand, we may have been given a large bonus before we left the office to join our lunch date who wants to help us to spend it, wrapping her sparkling eyes, expressions of love and promises of good times in the suggestion of an early trip to Mauritius. All of this, combining to stimulate our positive emotions, would delight us, quite possibly leading to acts of procreation in fulfilment of our genes' ultimate needs?

UNBORN CHILD: Yes. But there is more to it than that. Because, as you suggest, unique to emotional beings, there is love, which is not only an emotion itself but the very glue that holds you all, and all that we are considering, together. Love is the only voluntary emotion you have; that is, one you can choose to give or withhold. When it is added to the equation – more particularly the need to be loved, which is your greatest need of all, and the force that can make life feel like magic – what may have appeared theoretical then takes on a human edge and becomes very real indeed.

5

The Unborn Child

The sight or sound of another human being is the most physically arousing thing that a human being can see or hear.

SUSAN QUILLIAM (b. 1950)
Body Language: Actions Speak Louder than Words (2004)

UNBORN CHILD: 'Am I loved?'

AUTHOR: Are you loved? Why, of course you are. Come on, you were conceived through an act of love. As an unborn child your needs are provided for in their entirety. You are shielded and protected from all outside harm whilst being nurtured and cared for. In fact, you could say that your present situation is the epitome of love, the embodiment of loving, indeed, you know of no other existence but loving. Your survival depends upon it and one day you will love in return. So, yes, you are totally loved.

UNBORN CHILD: Ah, but 'Am I loved?' is not my question. It's yours, the question every single human being who has ever lived asks of themselves every day, in truth many, many times every day, as I shall explain.

Let me start with other people. You meet them all the time, strangers on the metro or in the street, colleagues in your place of work, people you deal with generally or as part of your job, friends you have lunch with or loved ones at home or on holiday, people you come across whilst travelling. You see and spend time with these people all the while, but do you realise that, when all is said and done, there is nothing as arousing for you in all the world as another human being? It means that, suspended between birth and death on this tiny planet in the vastness of the universe, nobody has to feel alone, that despite everything, there is some unspoken bond between everyone simply because you are human beings sharing the feeling of being alive. But, more than that, it means that at any one time, you are capable as human beings of belonging to one another. Born of the same strain of Creation, you have the ability to banish each other's loneliness and help each other to fulfil your needs; in other words you can look to one another for help, especially in terms of assisting each other to survive, of protecting your genes and passing them on.

This form of inter-dependence provides us with a definition of love. For love is nothing if not a form of dependency, a dependency of care. When you love, you care for someone else. When someone loves you, they care for you. When you need love, what you actually need is to find the care or love of another human being.

It is love that truly distinguishes human beings from other animals. It is love that is supreme above all your emotions; love indeed that holds the key to happiness and fulfilment. Love is for sharing, it is a giving and receiving, its absence the source of all your sorrows.

But there is more to love, for it is love that will reveal the answers that we are seeking. Love is the life-force within all human beings, distinguishing them from other species.

AUTHOR: Are you saying that everything boils down to love?

UNBORN CHILD: Please wait. I have little time and much to tell you. Let me deal with human troubles. Do you find that despite everything you know about love, life lets you down, as it turns out not to be as simple or as good as it should be? You nod, but what do you expect when your personal responses to all experience are beyond both your understanding and your control? You function, you exist but you drown in the Speechless Real. The Speechless Real places scales upon your eyes and you never see, you're not even aware of needs, senses, powers that are yours and are meant to help you make sense of life. Instead, you merely drown in confusion.

Do you know what it is, the Speechless Real? It's all the things I have yet to see: the frailties, inadequacies, insecurities, excesses, limitations, unkindnesses, excuses, jealousies and cruelties that have become the everyday realities of navigating life. The Speechless Real envelops you, preventing you from seeing life, how it could be and why it is not as it ought to be. When I am born it will envelop me but, now, before birth, I can see everything with crystal clarity.

Back to my question 'Am I loved?' You ask that question of yourselves in response to the greatest of all your needs, the need to be loved.

That need begins as early in the cycle of life as me. Consider my situation. It is not unlike that of genes riding through time as passengers within our bodies. Like them I am entirely dependent for survival upon the body that carries me, that is my mother. Like our genes, I am helpless but, nevertheless, I am secure in my dependency.

You see, a mother's love, like a person's emotions, provides for my survival whilst, after birth, the care of those I will depend on will continue to safeguard my protection. And so it is that love helps me to survive just as one day it will help me to procreate. Love satisfies my primal needs, it protects my genes, it protects me and it will eventually help me to pass my genes on, as the bearer of Life to my children.

Love looks out for the dangers you must avoid to survive. Love is another pair of eyes and ears, a source of care, a wise and experienced hand to avoid risk, and love is a source of happiness too, the most necessary gift to Humankind.

But above everything else, giving love to someone satisfies the other's need to be loved. As with genes finding protection in your emotions, when you are loved you find both protection and fulfilment in the emotions of others.

AUTHOR: So the emotions of others can protect our genes?

UNBORN CHILD: Certainly, but I may have less time than you think so, please, let me go on. Here is the crux of all human existence. Putting aside the conflicting emotions, misunderstandings and confusions that are the Speechless Real, what does everyone want? Well, it's simple. All any human being wants, all every human being actually longs for, is to be loved.

This will be as true for me as it is true for you, as true for my children as for yours, and it applies to everyone with equal force from the greatest saint to the most evil tyrant.

AUTHOR: Even the Hitlers and the Saddams of this world?

UNBORN CHILD: Particularly them. Had they felt genuinely loved it is very unlikely that they would have behaved with such terrible inhumanity. By not feeling loved they became inhuman, acting in a way that was outside the bounds of humanity.

You see, even more than loving, needing to be loved is as much part of the human condition as Elizabeth Barrett Browning's 'breath, smiles, tears'. That need, that dependency on others, when you thought yourself so strong and self-sufficient, exists whether you are aware of it or not, can speak of love or have difficulty in finding it, or spend your life in search of it. Everyone needs to be loved even if they are unlovable.

That is why I ask the question 'Am I loved?' It is the essence of every human being, the single factor that all human beings share, the greatest leveller this side of death. Needing to be loved is genuinely your all-consuming need, its fulfilment or otherwise serving as a barometer for your mental health, its satisfaction essential to your wellbeing.

AUTHOR: You seem to be getting a little flushed. Would you like to take a break?

UNBORN CHILD: No, thank you. There is more to tell you. The main thing I still have to explain.

If you have an overwhelming need to be loved, you also have an obvious need to check on how that need is being fulfilled. And so you have a separate sense just for that.

I'll tell you about this sense and you'll see how knowing about it breathes life into your need to be loved, indeed into you and every human being after aeons of sterile misunderstanding. No-one seems to know about it and yet the sense is all-present, as constant in your make-up and as crucial to the way that you function as your other senses of sight, hearing, smell, taste and touch. It remains supreme over them all. No, really, this is true. But… just listen.

This sense has always been part of Humankind, exposed to all human dealings, and yet it has never been identified as part of the human make-up. Unique to Humankind, it is absolutely fundamental to the way that human beings exist and function, affecting their lives on every conceivable level. More yet than that, it makes sense of all human problems, providing an explanation for the ones affecting you and those that have afflicted Humankind throughout the ages.

So what is it? Let us go back to your emotions. Remember, they serve to protect your genes. But as your emotions don't strictly originate with you and cannot be controlled by you, how do you process them? How do you respond to them and accommodate them within your being?

'Am I loved?' The answer is the question. That question is the most asked question of all time because it is used to interpret your emotions. The sense that no-one is aware of applies that single question to all of your emotions, processing them by reference to the effect that they have on your all-important need to be loved. For everything that happens to you, every experience you will ever have, is processed on the basis of how your emotions impact, either positively or negatively, on your personal need to be loved.

This is the absolute feeling of all humanity. The private sense of self, of identity, of you, of how you see and experience life and how you assess every situation you are ever exposed to. Simply, 'Am I loved?' No wonder Humankind is the only 'I' apart from God.

This is how human beings function. Here is your unknown sense interpreting the language of your emotions. Your emotions and your unknown sense are so totally intertwined that all life is experienced by reference to the effect that your emotions have on your need to be loved. Whether people are aware of it or not, the degree to which that need is satisfied will determine their entire response to every experience of being human and alive, providing a private register of experience that is separate and unique to every individual.

Consider what this means. Every single aspect of your life registers with you emotionally and, through that, impacts on your need to be loved. Just as your emotions are classified as either positive or negative, so your need to be loved is affected either positively or negatively by your emotions.

And so, your life is spent converting human experience into feelings of being loved or not loved. In this way, and probably without your realising it, an emotion will either make you feel loved or it will make you feel unloved, affecting your feelings, your mood and, over time, your character.

Feeling loved is what being human boils down to. The ultimate prize of human existence, it is the only way you can ever feel whole and happy and at peace with yourselves.

AUTHOR: What's wrong, little man, are you OK?

UNBORN CHILD: It's... beginning. I can feel... it's... oh dear. I'm not at all finished. There is so much more.

AUTHOR: No! Please don't go. Please don't...

The magic is spent. The Unborn Child is approaching birth much like an old man approaching death. His time has simply run out. The wise and tiny unborn president is gone, gone before we can thank him or say farewell, gone before we can kiss him goodbye and wish him good luck, his image fading into the confusion that enfolds us all, so that he can breathe and live, pray and struggle, like the rest of us.

But our experiment has been a triumph. Magic and innocence have combined to slay the Speechless Real and we now have a comprehensive overview of the human condition. All will be amplified and explained in the remaining chapters, particularly our Supreme Sense ('the sense that no-one knows of') that contains more wonder than our little friend had time to tell us of. With the removal of the encumbrance on our understanding that was the Speechless Real, we are free to proceed with our study.

6

Genes, the Riddle and
the Wheel of Life

Fleet Street has a very animated appearance,
but I think the full tide of human existence is
at Charing Cross.

SAMUEL JOHNSON (1709–84)
quoted in JAMES BOSWELL (1740–95)
The Life of Samuel Johnson (1791), Vol. 2

There is an ancient fable borne on the winds of time. Heaven knows where it originated or how it reached us. Perhaps it came out of Africa with migrating *Homo sapiens*.

The Fable begins in the mellow, golden light of a late summer's afternoon in the shrinking, drought-ridden forest in Africa that we encountered in Chapter One, with the same tree-ape falling out of the same tree.

But what our tale did not explain, and what the Fable tells us, is that the tree-ape's inglorious exit from the tree, and subsequently from the forest, was witnessed both by God and by Nature, who were immersed, at the time, in a deep and important conversation in the very forest with which we are concerned. What makes the Fable quite wonderful is that the conversation was of crucial significance to us as it marked the first tenuous steps towards our evolution as emotional human beings.

Here is the Fable told in its original style, which I hope you will be able to follow:

And God said to Nature: 'Behold the creatures that we have made: the fish of the sea, the fowl of the air and every living thing that creepeth upon the Earth, and these tree-apes too, have neither the capacity to enquire of today, nor to ponder on yesterday, nor to think of tomorrow. These tree-apes and all the rest of creation exist but to pass on life to the next generation and for no other purpose.'

And Nature said. 'It is true, O Lord, that all the creatures that have been created are but stepping stones for Life, on Life's great journey to eternity.'

God's countenance grew dark. 'But there is more to life than keeping the spark of Life alive,' he said. 'Shall not life itself have a purpose, enabling beings, one day, to become as precious to us as the Life that they bear?'

But Nature did not comprehend God's vision and replied thus: 'What greater purpose can there be, O gracious Lord, than to keep the spark of Life alive?'

And God said: 'It is time to make man after our likeness, to create a conscious being unlike all others, one who may smile and laugh and cry; a thinker who may learn to reason and imagine, who has a conscience and may dream. An individual who may love, feel compassion, communicate and speak; whose brain may open up fantastic possibilities, whose emotions will give both feeling and purpose to his days; one whose greatest needs shall be to love and be loved, that he may be happy and his days may be long upon the earth.'

Now Nature, through whom all Creation had evolved, was sore perplexed. Because never before had God called upon her to create a particular creature; the fish of the sea and the fowl of the air and every living thing that creepeth upon the earth, verily all creatures in which there is a breath of Life, had evolved one from another over time as the seasons had turned into years and the years into ages.

And so, Nature answered God, saying: 'My dear and ever gracious Lord, how wilt thou make this man you speak of? From what shall man be fashioned? There is not a creature in the world who hath a mind to enquire nor even language to speak, nor yet desire to do anything but that it did yesterday, with thoughts neither of change nor of improvement, nor of what the morrow shall bring.'

Now, as Nature spoke, behold, there was a mighty crash and a branch upon which sat a tree-ape did break, for the tree was brittle from want of rain. And a terrible cry went up from the tree-ape, a cry so great that it stilled the noise of the forest. For the tree-ape had fallen from a great height, and the dust created from the impact as the ape hit the ground was such that it appeared as if he had been swallowed up in it and disappeared.

'Man shall evolve like the rest of creation, but man shall have a brain like no other. A brain is the answer,' declared the Lord. 'A brain so great that there shall be nothing to compare it to in all the universe. And emotions too, man shall have emotions to give feelings to man, and a mind, man shall have a mind where his emotions may contend with reason, and man's mind shall be a well of conscious thought. And to man shall I give dominion over the fish of the sea and over the fowl of the air and over every little thing that creepeth upon the Earth.'

Now as the tree-ape fell out of the tree, he had landed on a column of ants entering the forest. And some of the ants were thrown up into the air, but such ants did quickly fall back to earth. Behold, as the dust settled the mate and two offspring of the ape were patting and comforting him and cooing, as he lay stricken on the ground, whilst the ants that had fallen back to earth continued on their way.

And Nature remembered the primal needs of every living being to survive and procreate, which needs she had supported by instincts and sensations provided to all Creation, to ensure that the miracle of Life that Creation carried would be passed onto the next generation.

And so, Nature answered unto God: 'O great and beneficent God, there are few creatures yet with emotions save those like the tree-apes, with larger brains. Such beings have emotions merely to supplement the instincts with which their lives are ordered, the better to protect the life-force that is within them and is the source of Life itself. But, dear Lord, therein lies a danger. With brains so large, and emotions so profound, shall not man have freedom and volition sufficient to order his own days? Peradventure, the course of man's life shall not be guided by instinct and sensation as are other lives, shall not the life-force that is within him be put at risk? For man shall have become a god without concern for the order of Creation or the preservation of Life from one generation to another. Indeed man may live for the day or the moment, ungoverned by instincts of survival and procreation by which all Creation is bound.'

Now the tree-ape that had fallen out of the tree was covered in dust and was greatly afflicted and sore hurt. But with much pain he slowly rose up from the dust in the afternoon light, as his family cooed and sought to assist him.

'Nature, Nature, we shall proceed to make man and, lo, this is how it shall be done. Man shall be created with a brain like no other so that he shall have dominion over all the earth. As companion to his brain shall he have emotions sufficient to enable his spirits to plunge as deep as the deepest ocean and to soar as high as a shooting star; but, hearken, dear Nature, his emotions shall be committed to his life-force, by which he shall be formed, protecting its needs as surely as instincts protect the life-force of all other creatures. Fashioned thus, the seed of man shall assuredly pass through the generations. When man lives in harmony with his emotions, his spirit shall be at peace. Now, how shall this man be brought forth?'

'My dear and ever generous Lord,' Nature answered, as with much distress the tree-ape that had fallen out of the tree began to limp away from the forest towards the parched grasslands, his mate and their young by his side. 'There are the hominids here, the tree-apes nearly distinct from other primates. They are sturdy and strong and have emotions enough to grow with their brain.'

'Behold, this is very good,' God said. 'We shall proceed in creating man. He shall be to us a being to be blessed, that he may be fruitful and multiply and replenish the earth.'

'From the apes that live in the trees?' Nature asked.

'No,' said the Lord, as the tree-ape at last reached the grasslands. 'From the tree-ape that has fallen out of the tree.'

This is all we have of the Fable. Whether there is more we do not know. As it comes to an end the tree-ape slopes off to commence four million years of evolution that will see his brain triple in size; four million years in which, very gradually, he will become human, metamorphosing into the first and, so far, the only species of emotional being. As *Homo sapiens*, the thinking species, we look at our tree-ape astonished at the thought that we could have directly descended from him.

But we did. Evolution is nothing if not genetic change, and 320,000 or so generations were sufficient to effect the genetic change that transformed a tree-ape into a human being, a hominid sitting vacantly in a tree thinking about food into a vital human being thinking and talking about food – and sex, and power, and self, and everything else under the sun; 320,000 generations to fashion the greatest brain in Creation, an unimaginably complex organ of far greater potential than the rather limited use we make of it, with a companion range

74

of emotions capable, as God proposed in the Fable, of plunging our spirits as deep as the deepest ocean and of letting them soar as high as a shooting star.

Just as President Clinton won election by concentrating on the maxim 'It's the economy, stupid', in Nature it is always the genes that count. Standing between Nature and Creation, between the unknown and the known, genes are the very linchpin of all Creation, bringing Life to Creation and Creation to Life.

Inhabiting a parallel universe to our own, feeling nothing, caring for nothing and intending nothing save their own preservation, genes exist beyond our senses. We do not feel them, we are not aware of physically carrying them, but as the architects and builders of Creation they are the sine qua non of all existence. Life may be Nature's most treasured and precious creation and the host bodies of Creation her greatest triumph, but ultimately both Life and Creation are wholly dependent upon genes for survival.

For genes are the message and it is the message that counts, whilst what happens to those who propagate it is of little relevance. And so, passing through microscopic sperm and egg, genes are the recipe for making and bringing every host body to life.

Imagine what this means as we watch an embryo, then a foetus, then a baby, an infant, a child, an adolescent develop, changing in physical and mental terms almost as substantially as had the tree-ape to become a human being. And imagine how our genes continue to regulate our body, preserving the life within us until the day that we die.

If we die without progeny our genes will die with us. But if we have children, some will live on through them. With each child born the gene pack is shuffled, with fifty per cent of each parent going to create the child. In this way genes continue for millions of years, becoming all but immortal. But they do not evolve, merely surviving or failing to survive in a gene pool. It is the gene pool that evolves. Crucially – and perhaps this is hard to understand – host bodies exist for the benefit of their genes rather than the other way around.

Extraordinary as it may seem, Charles Darwin went to his grave unaware of the existence of genes, although he attempted to reconcile heredity and evolution in *On The Origin of Species*. The word 'gene' did not even appear in our dictionaries until 1913, but genes themselves have ever been with us, arising when that original single-celled organism hosted the very first spark of life. Since then, all thanks to genes, Life has enveloped the globe.

Genes are the miracle within us, the apparent magic that we can never fully understand, existing simply to provide Life with host bodies to ferry her on her way to Eternity. We have no idea why this should be so, but everything we are concerned with, everything about our world, everything about ourselves, stems from this great truth.

Our genes' concern to survive enables our own survival. Far from being a selfish desire, as propounded by Richard Dawkins, that concern is essential to fulfil Nature's purpose, enabling Life to continue on its journey through successive generations. For genes have no alternative but to be faithful to Nature and her scheme for Creation. If they were not faithful, life would simply come to an end. And so, in my respectful view, genes are more aptly described as faithful than selfish.

Genes have brought life to Creation so that every living creature, being or thing might be a bearer of Life. Again, in my opinion, 'bearer of Life' seems a more relevant description than Richard Dawkins's 'survival machine' as it is entirely consistent with Nature's fundamental concern to protect and perpetuate the life that animates us.

For bearing Life is what Creation does. And just as importantly, it is all that Nature intends Creation to do. And Creation is able to do it solely because of Nature's genes.

Having explained the role genes play in the preservation of Life, we come now to the essential question of how our genes themselves are protected. We come to the Riddle.

But first, we must return to the Fable because there is more to it than you might think. Because whilst you may not have appreciated it, the Fable not only introduces us to the Riddle, it actually solves it before we have properly defined it in these pages!

The question behind the Riddle is one that many people will have pondered at some time or other. What are our emotions for? And why are we unable to understand or control them?

To my chagrin, comprehensive answers to these questions were also provided by the Unborn Child before I had the opportunity to explain them. But if you did not pick them up then the Fable has probably enabled you to work them out, for it expresses the matter very well: 'His emotions shall be committed to his life-force [i.e. his genes], by which he shall be formed, protecting its needs as surely as instincts protect the life-force of all other creatures.' In other words, our emotions are to be committed to the protection of our genes.

Elsewhere in the Fable, the question is asked: 'With brains so large, and emotions so profound, shall not man have freedom and volition sufficient to order his own days?' Due to our volatile character, imagination, huge brains and freewill, Nature does not trust us to protect our genes ourselves. And so our emotions are commandeered to protect our genes and the Life we carry.

How does this work? By a measure of the most sublime and ineffable genius.

How else may we describe a situation in which, entirely without our knowledge, understanding or consent, our emotions, the very faculties through which we exist as emotional beings, constantly processing all human experience, are co-opted for the protection of our genes?

This means that our emotions, which we always believed were ours to order, respond entirely to the needs of our genes rather than serving our personal needs as we would understand them. It means no less than that our emotions have been hijacked or suborned, call it as you will, for the greater protection of Life, preferring the needs of our genes to our own personal and human needs.

The preservation of our genes is thus confirmed as the defining rationale of our existence. For our emotions are irrevocably tied to the survival of our genes as surely as are the instincts and sensations of much of the rest of the animal kingdom tied to the survival of theirs. And, for the greater security of us all, our emotions respond to the needs of our genes even when, as a result, Humankind is quite unable to handle those emotions.

It will require us understanding the Trick and our Supreme Sense before we will be able to feel more comfortable living with our emotions, but we have solved the Riddle. In doing so we are now in a position to discover one of Nature's greatest secrets. Consider the following statements, all of which are self-evident from our consideration of genes:

LIFE *powers* GENES
GENES *fuel* INSTINCTS (and EMOTIONS)
INSTINCTS (and EMOTIONS) *protect* GENES
GENES *preserve* LIFE

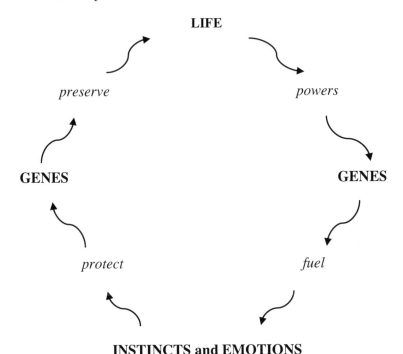

LIFE

preserve   *powers*

GENES   **GENES**

protect   *fuel*

INSTINCTS and EMOTIONS

Just four lines, four nouns and four verbs comprising the secret of life. Our caveman may have been the first human being to invent the wheel, but, convert these lines into a diagram and you will see that Nature got there first. For here is a comprehensive explanation of how Life is preserved and perpetuated in every single host body in Life's journey through time.

This is how Life is preserved through genes; how genes are protected by instincts and emotions; how instincts and emotions are fuelled by genes; how genes, in turn, are powered by Life. We have found the perpetual cycle of Creation, where Life is supreme, its preservation both paramount and eternal.

Nothing could be more simple or ingenious. This is how Creation works and has always worked, the only complexity being that everything in these four short lines and this diagram is invisible.

It is therefore impossible to witness the Wheel of Life as it turns, the secret of life whilst it works. It is like the wind rearranging a pile of leaves: we cannot see the wind save for how it causes the leaves to dance and fly.

We are the leaves to Nature's wind, our individual fates and experiences like so many leaves, as varied as the billions of creatures, beings and things that bear Life. But ever invisible and perpetually in motion, the great Wheel of Life is both eternal and inviolate.

As long as we survive, our genes will survive, but they do so because of their great partnership with our emotions that protect them.

At what cost we shall now see.

7

Emotions

*As you pass the tender years of youth into harsh and
embittered manhood, make sure you take with you on
your journey all the human emotions! Don't leave them
on the road for you will not pick them up afterwards.*

NIKOLAI GOGOL (1809–1852)

Dead Souls (1842)

*Do you know what 'Le vice anglais' – the English vice
– really is? Not flagellation, not pederasty – whatever
the French believe it to be. It is our refusal to admit
our emotions. We think they demean us, I suppose.*

TERENCE RATTIGAN (1911–77)

In Praise of Love (1973)

Believe it or not, this world is one huge self-service restaurant where one species will dine on another, always with an eye open for other species who may wish to dine on them.

Life in the world around us makes for a perilous existence. Our world is populated by millions of species and billions of creatures. However microscopically small or insignificant some of them may be, every creature is a bearer of Life. Every creature lives according to its nature and yet a very considerable proportion are destined to become the innocent prey of other creatures.

For on earth there is a food chain. One creature needs to eat another merely to survive. It represents a kind of culling by encouraging the survival of the fittest. Slightly fascistic in nature, the survival of the fittest serves not only to feed the population of the planet but also to prune out the weakest, thereby improving gene pools. Species are rarely extinguished as dog eats dog or, more precisely, lion eats gazelle, crocodile eats zebra, fox eats rabbit, bird eats worm, spider eats fly and Humankind hunts, farms and rears animals simply to feed on them.

So, when we speak of survival in the animal kingdom we often mean creatures surviving the ravages of one another. After all, even the Children of Israel were sent quail to eat before manna was provided for them from Heaven. But there is no manna to feed the teeming life on earth. Every creature has to provide for itself, even if this involves taking the Life that Nature deems so precious and goes to such trouble to preserve and protect.

We could well ask: how could creation survive if it were not feeding on itself? But then, what does this say about the sanctity of Life?

We are left with a paradox. On the one hand Life is protected within all Creation by needs and instincts to survive and procreate, such needs and instincts presumably being deemed sufficient at least until Life has been passed onto the next generation. On the other, it is obvious that, all along, one creature's Life-bearing body was intended to become another creature's lunch.

In distinction to God, nobody ever goes to war for Nature. Nature has no emotional content, yet it is almost as if she has some sense of fair play, as having ostensibly done everything possible to protect Life within all Creation, she has also endowed Creation with a further gift. A gift to provide each creature with a final chance to survive, so that its perishing at the paws and jaws of another creature would be down to bad luck or fate, rather than a defect in its design.

The gift is fear, which will bring us to our emotions. In short, Nature has endowed the majority of the animal kingdom with a sense of fear, in the form of responses which serve the same purpose as our fear emotion in Humankind.

As Gavin de Becker explains in his riveting book *The Gift of Fear*, fear is a survival signal that sounds in the presence of danger. Unlike other emotions it is a signal that is intended to be very brief, but it is an emotion whose purpose is to alert us to danger threatening the protection of our genes and therefore the Life that we bear.

Fear is a servant of intuition, a remnant of our original emotions which were purely instinctual by nature, causing bodily reactions designed to serve in times of danger to help us to protect our genes and therefore to keep people alive. By bypassing the brain through the amygdala, fear causes beneficial physiological changes and bodily responses even before we have had time to think. In this way, it makes us concentrate on the danger confronting us, enabling us quickly to assess options: our senses quicken, getting us physically ready for coping with danger with increased blood flow (for fighting and running), release of cortisol (to help blood coagulate more quickly in case of injury) and lactic acid (heating up in the muscles to prepare for effort), focused vision, and increased heartbeat and breathing to support all these symptoms and, inevitably, to help us run away.

Most animals, even though destined to be killed and eaten, or eaten and killed, are protected by fear responses. It follows that the early human beings who were most afraid were probably the ones most likely to survive and consequently those from whom we are descended.

How strange that with Nature making such provision to protect Life, the world should become such a cruel and dangerous place. But Humankind has no rivals when it comes to cruelty. Compared to Creation at large, human brutality towards fellow human beings is in a class of its own.

When equipped with magnificent brains, brilliant minds and keen intelligence, all gloriously enhanced by a huge repertoire of emotions, why do we behave as we do, fighting, going to war, murdering, robbing, raping, plundering and committing unspeakable atrocities so regularly that they barely make the news? Tragically, we do so because of our emotions, the very things we function by – or, more to the point, because we are the victims of emotions which we do not understand and are unable to control. But we shall soon discover how, with emotions serving as the currency for all our dealings, human existence has been blighted by not understanding or being able to handle them.

Of course, it will be said that not every conflict can be reduced to the inability to handle our emotions. But, in truth, practically all conflicts have an emotional basis. With any conflict the temperament of the principal parties is hugely relevant, because, depending upon the circumstances, the chances are that they will be driven by negative emotions, which, whilst designed to help us to survive, can be all that is required to fan the flames of conflict and potential disorder.

We are emotional beings and we experience the world through our emotions. To illustrate this there is a story that may be apocryphal but makes the point, concerning Hitler and Wittgenstein, the philosopher.

Born within a week of each other in 1889, apparently they were at boarding school together. Hitler's background was relatively humble and uncultured whereas Wittgenstein came from a wealthy and cultivated family, and was Jewish. The story goes that Hitler took great offence at something Wittgenstein had done or said to him and that this led to his becoming a rabid anti-Semite.

Such is the genesis of disaster, how emotions can shape history.

Factor in hate, jealousy, insecurity, outrage and prejudice, and we have a recipe for practically all the many international conflicts and problem areas at the present time. Think Syria, Lebanon, Iraq, Egypt, Libya, Yemen, Bahrain; think Turkey, Iran, Al Qaeda, Hezbollah, ISIS, Hamas; think Middle East peace; think Ukraine, Belarus, Russia, China, Thailand; think North Korea, Burma, Cuba, Venezuela; think India, Pakistan,

Afghanistan, Sudan, Mali, Rwanda, the Central African Republic, Nigeria, Uganda, Congo; think Hitler, Stalin, Mao, Pol Pot, Saddam, Assad, Gaddafi; think terrorism, xenophobia, race riots, immigration; think bullying, relationship breakdowns, child abuse, domestic violence and the sheer competitiveness of modern life. The list is endless and it is timeless.

Think of how emotions colour opposing views, supporting aggression, conflict, a faith, a belief, an ideal, a cause, a pattern of behaviour, and you will come face to face with the inordinate role that emotions play in conflicts and inter-personal problems.

Outside the legal system (and often within it) most conflicts, be they national, international or domestic, or between individuals, religions, tribes, groups or political parties, will have as their origin a failure to handle personal emotions. This is why understanding and being able to handle our emotions is so vitally important; why our ignorance of the human condition is so challenging; and yet, in perhaps the ultimate irony, neither one of these failures to understand our make-up induces the necessary fear within us to make us aware of this particular danger.

Stop here, with the progress we have made so far with the Riddle, and we emerge as complicated, unstable, incomplete and imperfect, as vulnerable, uncertain victims of our emotions. But stop here, and you will see Humankind as it is today and as it has always been, wholly dependent upon its emotions, and yet pitifully unaware of how to understand or to handle them.

But do let us stop here. It is time for a change of mood.

'I left your body to return to your soul!' These most chilling words are spoken towards the end of A *Dybbuk*, a powerful, brilliant but disturbing play written in 1920 by S. Ansky. Concerned with the spirit of a recently dead young man taking possession of a woman on the eve of her marriage to another man, the play must have had an added poignancy when first performed, as the author had himself died just two weeks before.

The woman, Leah, had been promised to the young man by her father whilst still a child but now, a *dybbuk*, the spirit of her long-forgotten betrothed, will not relinquish her. Having taken possession of her, the *dybbuk* takes over her being like a bad mood that keeps getting worse.

Leah behaves 'as if something got into her', writhing and groaning, her voice simulating the deep, anguished moan of the dead man. She becomes unrecognisable, appearing deranged, speaking as her lover, shedding all restraint, losing all resemblance to herself.

The *dybbuk* refuses all admonitions to go. Exorcism is applied in a terrifying, overwhelming and exhausting religious ritual, but, despite the desperate suffering it causes Leah, the spirit resists, refusing to quit her body on pain of eternal excommunication.

At length, however, the exhortations prevail. The tormented spirit is banished from Leah's body as, utterly exhausted, her strength entirely spent, she collapses to the ground. A circle is chalked around her so as to keep the *dybbuk* away as Leah lies, unconscious, prostrate, but safe.

And then in a shocking climax, with peace apparently restored, the calm is suddenly shattered as the voice of the *dybbuk* proclaims: 'I left your body to return to your soul.' Very gently Leah rises to join with her betrothed in a tight embrace, united in spirit for evermore. And then, she dies.

Is it possible that emotions are our personal *dybbuk*? For we are possessed of emotions as surely as Leah was possessed by the *dybbuk*. We are possessed of them as surely as if they had entered our souls.

As we have seen, responding exclusively to the need of our genes for the preservation of Life, rather than to our personal needs as we would construe them, emotions come out of nowhere, causing us to act or react, to behave in a manner that we might not have chosen for ourselves. No longer just the physiological changes and bodily responses they began as, emotions are our very essence as emotional beings. We function through them. They define us as human beings. Indeed, they have entered our soul, determining our entire experience of being human from the mundane to the sublime, from our daily intercourse with each other to our relationship with God.

Emotions are things that happen to us, they are not things that we can cause to happen. They can drive us mad, bring us to despair, wreaking harm, havoc and embarrassment, and yet, bringing depth, passion, value, experience, quality and sensitivity to life, they are the best things that we have. They are the source of all our feelings. Without them, life would be unimaginably bland and cold; indeed, it would be devoid of all essential passions that make us human and life worthwhile.

Without them, we would no longer be emotional beings, we would no longer have a soul.

But, serving to protect the Life within us, they are beyond our control. The best that we can do is to try to control our reactions to their expression by the suppression of anger or the masking of sadness or surprise. That is the only way we know how to handle them notwithstanding all the therapies, counselling and self-help books that may tell us otherwise.

Remember, Nature's overriding concern is to preserve Life. Emotions will do whatever it takes to protect our genes.

8

Loving Love

But I wasn't kissing her, I was whispering in her mouth.
CHICO MARX (1887–1961)

'I saw you take his kiss!' ''Tis true.'
'Oh modesty!' ''Twas strictly kept:
He thought I slept; at least I know
He thought I thought he thought I slept.'
COVENTRY PATMORE (1823–96) *The Kiss*

In 1971 the distinguished musician André Previn was a special guest star on the *Morecambe and Wise* show on British television. Eric Morecambe followed him to the piano to try to play the piece that Previn had just played.

His playing was a disaster.

'You're playing all the wrong notes,' Previn said.

'I'm playing all the right notes – but not necessarily in the right order,' Morecambe replied.

Those words sum up all one needs to understand about emotions and emotional problems.

Think of our emotions as musical notes. Think of a piano where each note on its keyboard represents a different emotion, with Love at middle C and Fear next to it, positive emotions to the right of Love and negative emotions to the left of Fear. What kind of music would we have a chance of making?

Between them, the notes cover all our moods and feelings, our aspirations and our deeds, our passions and our depressions, our expectations and our realities, our highs and our lows, and, much like a cloud liberated from night's oblivion by the illumination of the moon, this reflects our ever-changing pattern of experience. But it will not be us who play the notes, for our emotions arise unbidden outside our volition and control, and so the notes on the piano, their sound, their music, will play themselves as on a piano roll inside a pianola.

As often as not, like Eric Morecambe, they'll play the notes in the wrong order. Each time, each performance will be different and each performance will be as unique as the person whose emotions cover the keys. For the music is not ours to compose. We experience an emotion, a note is played, that is all. How the resulting sound will appear is anybody's guess. It could be happy, sad, rhapsodic, discordant, melodious, cacophonic, the notes could be long, they could be short, fast or slow, tuneful or atonal, major or minor in key.

It could be anything but predictable. For the price we pay for being emotional beings is having emotional problems. Here is the evidence. Every minute of every day we live with a constant flow of uninvited feelings, responding to all experiences, feelings that often bear opinions and demand reactions, feelings that, on reflection, may go against what we might think best. Living with such a complex, untamed force within us is sometimes like living with a stranger. Is it remotely surprising, therefore, that compared to other beings who have but the smallest emotional capacity or none at all, we are not at ease in ourselves and often find life frustrating and beset with problems? Will it be surprising if our piano playing sounds so unmelodious and harsh that we could never consider it to be music?

But will we accept that the sounds that offend us actually reflect what is going on inside us?

Before we abandon or destroy the piano, let us ask if we could design emotions differently so that we could control them, selecting each one before experiencing it. How would we go about it? How different would it be having emotions that we could control compared to those we have now? What difference would that make to our lives? What effect would this have on our world? Would it make it a safer, happier place and would our genes, with the Life that we bear, be more secure?

Let us retrace our steps up Sloane Street and the events on our imaginary walk that we posited to the Unborn Child. This all involved pre-ordained emotional responses to potential hazards even before there was time to think about what was happening. In this way we reacted automatically to being pushed off the pavement, being caught in the rain without an umbrella, being stood up for lunch, perhaps being mugged, sacked from our job or dumped by a girlfriend's text. We understood the feelings engendered by those happenings. We saw them as recognisable emotions, indeed as negative emotions, but they were already formed, not by our choice or conscious selection, but as instant reactions calculated to protect the Life within us, or, more specifically, our genes. They arose, moreover, as if our lives depended upon them, without giving us a chance to reject them or to select other emotional responses of our own.

Yes, we still have Stone Age emotions yet we live in a Cyberspace Age world, and yes, perhaps our emotions were perfected for a more primitive and violent era. However, we must understand that our emotional responses, albeit sometimes exaggerated, inappropriate or harmful, are not a sign that something is wrong, but precisely what we would expect from well-engineered emotions serving to protect our genes.

Nature does not take risks or chances. That is why we have our emotional armoury. And that is why our emotional responses are selected for us. Selecting them for ourselves would be akin to expecting people to remember to breathe. It could be done but it is most unlikely that anyone would survive the first twenty-four hours, especially if they intended to sleep.

And no, it would not be possible to invent new emotions. Our emotions cover the full gamut of all feelings and experiences. Our language confirms that this is so. Indeed it is inconceivable that we could even invent a new facial expression to partner a new emotion over and above those that we already universally share.

Our emotions are capable of responding to our personal needs as we would construe them only when, as may happen, the needs of our genes and those of ourselves will overlap. This will occur when we are in danger or wanting to make love, in which event our piano will play a passable tune.

Which brings us to love.

If fear is an emotion unlike all others, which lasts but a short time, then so is love, which can last for a lifetime. Love is different from other emotions. A composite of

- admiration
- affection
- approbation
- benevolence
- care
- compassion
- consideration
- desire
- devotion
- empathy
- esteem
- fondness
- friendship
- gratitude
- kindness
- need
- passion
- respect
- romance
- sympathy
- tenderness
- validation

love is the only emotion we can choose either to bestow or to withhold. There is no such thing as love when strangers' eyes meet across a crowded room; there is certainly attraction, probably lust, but not love. Love is a matter of choice. It is something we choose to give and, bearing in mind its lasting consequences, it is not something we should give lightly.

For good reason love is twinned with hope and optimism. When it comes, at first, life takes on a Panglossian aspect. Ours is the best of all possible worlds. We walk on air, our heart soars with our dreams, we obsess on thoughts of our beloved. When it ends life can feel as if it too has come to an end. But how does love begin? Love's messenger is a kiss, a thing of no use to one person but rapturously, deliciously, prized by two.

Over the centuries and millennia kissing has boomed, blossoming into a huge spectrum of varieties. The following short list, a selection of the many possible types of kisses, provides an insight into the intricacies and social conventions of kissing:

A mother's kiss, a father's, brother's, sister's kiss, a hand kiss, a ring kiss, a comforting 'there, there, it's alright' kiss, an air-to-air one–two–(three–four)-cheek kiss, a lascivious, passionate lover's kiss, a companionate and married kiss, a salivary, drink-filled, smelly kiss, a first, embarrassed, probing kiss, a goodbye kiss, a guilty, never explained kiss, a stolen kiss, a greeting, parting, living, loving kiss, a wondrous kiss-of-life kiss, the kiss of death, a very expensive bought kiss, a goodnight-but-call-me-tomorrow kiss, a goodnight-but-do-not-call-me-tomorrow kiss.

We all want to be kissed. We enjoy it very much. With Nature wanting us to survive, kissing is a sign of caring and protection. With Nature wanting us to procreate, a kiss is the first step to intimacy. The harbinger of love, kissing plays a key role in every relationship (although I have been told that many people in Laos in south-east Asia do not kiss at all). Its influence on human relations is wholly benign. Indeed, except, as the song says, that it can spread enough germs to cause pneumonia, nothing bad can be said of kissing.

Kissing is a human invention, and, by one of those massive and unexpected coincidences, we have already met the girl who first invented kissing; she was the woman or wife of our caveman who invented the wheel and called it a table. Of course, there were no conventions then for kissing, but whilst we might have expected her to plant the world's first kiss on her husband's lips it was actually given to somebody else!

Here is what happened.

By the warmth of a smoking camp fire melting the frost still white upon the ground, the young mother is nursing the infant we saw in her arms when her husband came home with a table. Snug in a bundle of skins and furs, the baby is taking his first solids. Weaning the child, the mother chews the food herself, grinding the venison into tiny morsels, mincing it between her broken teeth. And then, pushing back her matted hair, she feeds it to the child, gently nudging the food between her lips, the better to propel it with her tongue into the baby's expectant mouth held close to hers.

Just like a bird with a fat juicy worm to be shared amongst her young, here, at once, is an act of feeding, nurturing and loving. And here, in the birth of the kiss, is humanity's debut on Creation's cluttered stage.

Amidst the babble of sounds on that stage, kissing is the only language that practically every human being understands. A language without words, it is yet one which is universally spoken, celebrating at the same time the hopes, pleasures, misunderstandings and passions of love, and the absolute sameness of us all.

But kissing is only the start, the first bounding steps to love. Kissing is easy; it is the love it can lead to that causes problems.

Love can raise you up and pull you down as certainly as the untamed waves of the sea. Few people are fortunate enough to live with love yet none can live happily without it. Only a fool would claim to be able to fully understand love, let alone write about it, but as its absence from the hearts and lives of individuals is the primary cause of so vast a share of human misery, we must at least attempt to explain it.

There are more shades of love than colours, as many variations of love as people, yet, ultimately, be it romantic, companionate, familial or between friends, all love comes down to the same thing. But be warned, even love is seldom what it appears to be, as we shall see when we meet the Trick.

In a balcony scene to end all balcony scenes, the humour and sophistication of Edmond Rostand's *Cyrano de Bergerac* reminds us that Romeo and Juliet were at best adolescents. And yet the author can have had no inkling of how his most famous scene serves to mirror the undiscovered mirror of Nature.

It is night-time. The beautiful Roxanne stands in the dark upon a jasmine-covered balcony as she is wooed by a man in the garden below. She believes that she is listening to Christian, her suitor, who has the looks but not the tongue to deliver his message, whilst in fact it is Cyrano who speaks on Christian's behalf, having the tongue but, alas, not the looks to do it for himself, however much he might dream of doing so. In the epic translation of Anthony Burgess, the wooing is approaching its climax with these passionate words:

> *Each glance of your eyes begets some new*
> *virtue in me, new courage. Oh can you*
> *see this, feel it, understand? Do you sense*
> *my heart rising toward you in this intense*
> *stillness, whose perfumed velvet wraps us close?*

When the moon casts shadows over sleeping landscapes yet has no light of its own, and even the word 'romance' is defined as picturesque falsehood, be not surprised when love is not exactly what those engaged in giving and receiving it, in falling in it, deem it to be.

> *This night I speak, you listen. Never, in my most*
> *reckless unreasonable dreams, have I hoped for this.*
> *Now I am glad to die, knowing it is*
> *my words that make you tremble in the blue*
> *shadows of the tree.*

Cyrano is engaged in a subterfuge. But, however noble, true and dedicated love may be, it has an agenda of its own. Love, the most precious gift of Nature, unique to Humankind, is also love, the agent of Nature, devoted to one single and overwhelmingly important purpose – not the adoration of the one who receives it, but the protection of the Life that is within the one who gives it. It is love that is selfish, never our genes.

> *For it is true –*
> *You do tremble, like a leaf among the leaves,*
> *yes, and the passion of that trembling weaves*
> *a spider filament that seeks us now,*
> *feeling its way along the jasmine bough.*

Why? Because, like Milton Friedman's famous free lunch, love comes with strings attached. Love demands a bargain, something in return, the giving back of more love to make real Nature's Protection of Life through an additional mind, another pair of eyes and ears and hands, to watch out for the loved one. Roxanne responds:

> *Yes, I do tremble, and I weep and*
> *I am yours.*

Such is love requited, love complete. Love peaks when it is requited. Needing to be loved, the greatest, most basic need, shared by every human being the world over, is really but a call for someone to love us.

To us, this is an instinctive desire for fulfilment, whilst Nature sees it as a call for help, a call to find that other person who will share our kiss, our bed, our lives and provide protection to our existence. That, after all, is what everyone needs and wants so passionately: that our love may be requited, our love may be fulfilled, because someone loves us in return.

With love requited Nature's purpose is served. But more than that, with love requited it means that as human beings we are capable of belonging to one another with a sublime potential to help each other to fulfil our most private and personal needs.

In the next chapter we shall meet the Trick. It has nothing to do with the trick played by Cyrano and Christian on Roxanne, but it was always present, in the same velvet stillness of the blue shadows of the tree by Roxanne's balcony, if we had known to look for it.

9

Love and the Trick

I fear the Greeks even when they bring gifts.
VIRGIL (70–19 BC) Aeneid, Book 2

But what am I?
An infant crying in the night.
An infant crying for the light.
And with no language but a cry.
ALFRED, LORD TENNYSON (1809–92)
In Memoriam A.H.H. (1850)

What is commonly called love, namely the desire
of satisfying a voracious appetite with a certain
quantity of delicate, white human flesh.
HENRY FIELDING (1707–56) Tom Jones (1749)

'You should think twice about waking a dreaming child,' warns Dostoevsky's sometime mistress in J. M. Coetzee's *The Master of Petersburg*. We, and all humanity, are that dreaming child. However hardened sophisticated or even cynical we may be, our private dreams of love remain the single place of refuge that our thoughts can visit without fear of dashed hopes, betrayals, embarrassment or disappointment.

When we dream, we dream alone. When we awake, reality crowds in and our dreams, so vivid yet unreal, so unsuited to existence, are gone.

But waking the dreaming child will be different, for the reality that he will immediately face will be as fantastic as his dreams. He will awake, rubbing his eyes, and, seeing what we will show him, he will rub them again, staring at the large golden medallion before him. He will gaze in wonder: never in his young life will he have seen anything so beautiful, so rich and magic, so utterly exquisite.

His hand will reach to touch the medallion. Fashioned in 24-carat gold, it has a rococo relief of Cupid on one side and a jester with a face of Mr Punch engraved on the other. The Cupid is love as we all know and choose to believe it to be: poetry, songs, plays, literature, movies and letters celebrating love; the thrill of seeking love, the joy of finding and sharing it; our relationships and lifetime commitments based on love; having children and raising families through love; the heady, obsessive all-consuming passion of being in love; the timeless and enduring romance of love.

But if he turns the medallion over, and sees the Jester, the child will discover that love is not quite as noble and immaculate as we have always deemed it to be. Indeed, our conventional view of love will be shown, at best, to be imperfect and incomplete. For the reverse of the medallion is the other side of love. Not the mismatches, infidelities and broken-down relationships, not the misery, sadness, loneliness, despair and hatred of broken promises and vanished love, but something quite different, certainly unimaginable to the dreaming child, but something, indeed, that will come as a surprise to all dreamers and the bulk of Humankind.

Historically, the jester was the only person in a medieval court entitled to impart unpalatable truths to the monarch without risk of summary despatch. How fitting, therefore, that the reverse of the medallion should bear the image of a jester. Because the reverse of the medallion represents love from Nature's point of view.

We have observed that Nature sees things differently from ourselves. But, in truth, and in our ignorance, it is we who see things differently from Nature. Nature has a purpose in all that she does of which we are often completely unaware. She has an agenda in which our complex, busy lives are barely a footnote, a purpose and design that has passed us by.

Remember that Nature's sole and overriding concern is the protection and perpetuation of Life. And this she has achieved, subject only to natural disasters and human nature, by engineering us with our emotions and our capacity to love. In this way, we have the Riddle, with our emotions serving constantly to protect the Life within us by responding to the welfare of our genes rather than to our personal needs as we would see them.

Embracing our indefatigable need to be loved, we have love in the form of Cupid and the other side of love under the imprimatur of the Jester, and shortly we'll meet the Trick. All of these serve to protect and perpetuate life.

We shall come to these shortly, but first let us take a closer look at love to see how fundamental it is to us as human beings.

To put it simply, love is our predominant desire and our predominant need. Whether real or imaginary, preserved in print or clay, in film or writing or stored in the Cloud, or lost in the echoes of time, the stories of Humankind, whatever their plots, whoever their heroes or villains, whether they tell of good, evil, tragedy or farce, have but a single theme – all such stories will always come down to a variation of love.

Reducing life to its essential parts, stripping out the hosts of feelings that confront and confuse us every minute of every day, love is the single greatest force that influences and propels the course of all human experience. It is love that truly distinguishes us from other animals; it is love that makes life possible; indeed, it is love that makes life liveable and worthwhile.

And what is love? Love is like an elephant: you know it when you see it, even, or especially, when it is gone. But can love be defined? I think that it can. In fact, it comes down to something very simple, namely, the gauging and supply of another's needs. That is all it is.

It is a binding that contains us all, the glue that holds us together, the care, the security we crave for, the supply of our personal needs. In this way when we enter the world, love provides us with essential security and succour. In life it brings commitment and support to family and friends, unity, trust and companionship to partners and spouses. In death, love leaves us in grief, bereft for what we had but have no longer.

As we have seen, love is a composite of many lesser emotions and all of them are independently relevant to our discussions. Love encompasses all the virtues. It may prove to be transient or last a lifetime, or, as with our children, achieve a permanence from an irresistible pull from a genetic connection. In essence, as with our other emotions, love is protective of our genes. This is why tales of genes at risk, as in the most popular movies, appeal so strongly to our emotions.

We give love and we receive it. But, really, we trade it. We wish to love but, above all, we wish to be loved and in many instances that single desire will be greater than our personal desire to give love. Being loved, feeling loved, is the real and actual key to happiness, the answer to the age-old question: what makes people happy? As Steven Pinker writes in his superb *How the Mind Works,* 'the study of happiness often sounds like a sermon for traditional values. The numbers show that it is not the rich, privileged, robust or good-looking who are happy: it is those who have spouses, friends, religion and challenging work.' In short, all individuals whose relationships endow them with the potential to love and be loved.

Though with its infinite subtleties, passions, romance, tenderness, care and devotion, love ennobles Humankind, raising humanity high above all other creatures, its real purpose, as is always the case with Nature, is rather less rhapsodic than it might appear. When all the oaths are sworn, kisses kissed and hugs hugged, what is achieved once love is consummated is a package of genes to create a new generation. Love may be the food that nourishes our emotions, the jewel in the human crown, but, at the end of the day, the safe passage of Life to the next generation is what Nature requires and what Love delivers.

Which brings us to the reverse of the medallion, to the Jester, who understands how Nature has used love to gain her ends. For love is not only what everyone wants and desires and dreams of having, it is what everyone needs, with a force and direction that easily makes the need to be loved the greatest of all our many needs. That yearning, primordial, continuous and beautiful need is potentially the greatest unifier, the greatest leveller and the greatest life-force of all. We all share it and by giving love can potentially satisfy that need in others. But life isn't always so kind and, for many, its fulfilment is often left unsatisfied or not achieved.

Aspirations of love and of being loved are the constant waking schemes and sleeping dreams of all Humankind. Indeed, acting like a barometer for our mental health, the satisfaction or otherwise of our need to be loved is paramount for our wellbeing. Come back to Sloane Street, to our imaginary walk with the Unborn Child, and you will see our negative emotions kicking in when faced with threats to our wellbeing and comfort. Such emotions register for our protection and survival but also in reaction to events which undermine or threaten our feeling of being loved in its extended sense. Being stood up for lunch, sacked peremptorily or dumped by a girlfriend's text all detract from our need to be loved, causing our emotions to come to our aid much as if we had been physically at risk. Indeed, the resultant negative emotions explain many of the bad feelings experienced by people every day, even by events as innocent as someone pushing ahead of us in a line, or one of the many daily discourtesies that offend our dignity.

Because, when we feel loved, we feel both protection and fulfilment in the emotions of others. That need, that essential dependence on others when we consider ourselves strong and self-sufficient, exists whether or not we are aware of it, can speak of love, have difficulty in finding it or spend our lives in search of it. All of us need to be loved, even when we persuade ourselves that we don't or appear to be unlovable. Because, as we have said, needing to be loved is really just a call for someone to love us.

But there is very much more to our need to be loved than this. Needing to be loved produces its own tremendous energy. By providing us with a need to be loved, Nature helps us to mobilise our positive emotions to find or create love. This ensures the protection of Life when loving relationships are achieved.

Any way of living that is conducive to love will often be conducive to procreation. Nature loves a lover. But she is no sentimentalist. Having caused us to do her bidding, she has no care about whom we couple with or whether we are happy.

Very gently, the dreaming child is beginning to awaken. Consider this extract from *Shadows of the Hudson* by Nobel laureate Isaac Bashevis Singer.

Imagine there is a person who knows only one language – let's say Yiddish – and doesn't know of any other. Let's say Yiddish is dead, and that there is only one other person left who understands it. In that case, the one who knows only Yiddish will strain every fibre to follow him to the ends of the earth. That's the relationship between you and me. I can't talk to anyone but you.

It may feel as if love were all about something else, we may wish that it were, but however wonderful, devoted or tragic love may be, however urgent, lost, driven or helpless it may seem, after all the promises and pledges, commitments, tears and sleepless nights, love is only about one thing, it is about self-preservation, and that means survival.

Surviving is integral to love. It is what we try to do, what Nature has engineered us to do, so as to protect the Life we carry. And surviving is all that Nature asks of us. Rather than the great motivator, love, our passionate dispenser of promises, becomes our foremost protector. From all that we do, from seeking love to finding someone to have children with, to bringing those children up, the direction of our entire lives is aimed at surviving because survival is the magnetic pole of the human compass. Everything about us, from our emotions (remember the Riddle) to our wants, desires and dreams, to all of our needs, is concerned with survival; in social, emotional, practical, material, religious or political terms; from our family and the friends we choose, to the relationships we enter into, the career we pursue, the jobs we take, the homes we make, the religions we practise, even the political parties we vote for: ultimately everything comes down in one way or another to survival.

Taking love in its extended definition as a sum of its component emotions, as defined in Chapter Eight, we give love to find love, examining every situation we're in by reference to whether it makes us feel loved or not loved, since being loved, feeling loved, is our key to survival.

After Life itself, there is no greater force in all creation than our primeval need to hold onto it. Nature, therefore, equips us with the capacity to love, and it is this capacity that defines us as human, making us as we are, the only I apart from God. And so 'the sight or sound of another human being' becomes 'the most physically arousing thing that a human being can see or hear'. Such is the potential of love, going not just to our heart but to the heart of our being, the constant need for which provides us with our tenderest feelings, our romantic spirits, our passionate ways and a lifelong spur to go on.

Yet, even so, despite our many couplings, our experiences of love at first sight, our propensities to lust and self-delusion, love has, alone amongst the emotions, always been a matter of volition and choice. Indeed, although needing to be loved is our most solid aid to survival, love remains something we may bestow or withhold as we desire.

Or so we believe.

Humanity has never known where it was going and has thus been unable to find its way. But Nature has always known precisely where humanity was going. In spite of our beliefs in original sin, duty to God, liberty and freewill, it was going exactly where Nature led it!

A more apt term, perhaps, is 'enticed it'. For here is the Trick. Like the trail of Reece's Pieces that led the little alien out of the brush in *ET*, the need to be loved leads us through life by the nose just as if we were a donkey with an invisible carrot being constantly dangled before us. By endowing Humankind, in this way, with its ever-present need to be loved, Nature is forever enticing us towards love in all its myriad guises. Nature may not have achieved universal serenity and happiness, because love is not a hole and the need to be loved is not a golf ball waiting to drop snugly inside. But Nature has achieved a situation where everyone is programmed to seek love, and finding love is Humankind's ultimate goal. Because this in turn will lead, most likely, to the protection of Life and thus to survival.

Remember that survival, as we all know by looking at the world around us, is not necessarily living happily ever after; it is not necessarily being happy at all. It is merely living for long enough to pass one's genes onto the next generation.

And this is the Trick. By endowing Humankind with its perpetual need to be loved, in order to entice it to go where she wants it to go, Nature has employed the greatest carrot in all Creation. And in the process she has made donkeys of us all!

In some way it comes down to temptation. As a dog may be trained to sit up and beg with a treat, or a child may be bribed to behave in a supermarket by the promise of an ice cream, so Nature induces us to follow the only route she wants us to take by dangling the prospect before us of being loved. And so we chase our tails looking for love, because love will help us to protect our genes and pass them onto offspring.

It is as simple and as complicated as that. In nothing less than a triumph of basic psychology, aided immeasurably by the fact that she thought to make sex pleasurable and exciting, Nature fulfils her concern to provide a shelter for our life-bearing genes.

We have sex. The pleasure delivered is nothing less than Nature's ploy to get genes into the next generation. It worked with our ancestors, right back to the first human being, and it works with us. Sexual attraction bears the promise of love and happiness, hence the look shared between two strangers across a crowded room. It also explains why we tend to marry someone because we are attracted to their smile, their bottom, their navel or simply the colour of their eyes, in preference to our best friend, whom we like enormously, feel totally at ease with, and cannot stop talking to.

We are obsessed with being loved. Our need to be loved is both genuine and desperate, and by seeking love, sharing love, sampling love, testing love, we can find that extra source of care and protection. And through an act of love we can pass on our genes to the next generation.

That is all that Nature wants. That is how we conduct ourselves, how Nature programmes us to be. That we do so is our survival and Nature's Trick.

Stepping back from all we've considered, let us consider what Nature's Protections look like and how meticulously she has sought to preserve them whilst we who bear them enjoy relative freewill.

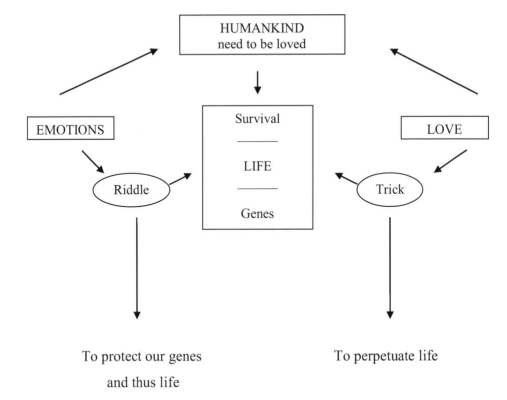

The diagram shows the protections put in place for Life. In addition to our emotions, it is through love that we will find protection for the Life within us, because love means survival to every one of us. Despite all our differences and antagonisms, the hate and violence, the hopes, suffering and despair that divide and threaten our world, our shared need to be loved must provide an unspoken bond between us. For we are all human beings sharing the experience of being alive, where the only burden from Nature is to protect the Life within us and to pass it on.

In our tragic, frightening times, could there be a finer potential for inter-dependence, or a better perspective on love? A forlorn hope but a worthy one.

The dreaming child is now awake and has grasped the shining medallion in both hands. We are, indeed, such stuff as dreams are made on, at once in need of being loved and only truly content when we give love and are loved in return. But gazing at the medallion, turning it over in his hands from Cupid to Jester to Cupid again, the child – and we with him – can now appreciate all that it represents, from need, to union, to the protection of Life and survival.

The medallion may be a symbol of love but it is also a statement of how love works and why.

10

The Supreme Sense

Men believe themselves free simply because they are conscious of their action and unconscious of the causes whereby their action is determined.
BARUCH SPINOZA (1632–77)

What is the answer?
(on receiving no response) *In that case, what is the question?*
GERTRUDE STEIN (1874–1946) last words

We have large brains. It is said that if each of our brain cells were a black London cab it would take an area greater than the size of western Europe to park them. Yet, however immense and powerful our brains may be, they are unequal to confronting the subtleties of the human condition. For whilst our brains are certainly big enough to cause problems, they are not necessarily big enough to solve them.

The consequence has been unfortunate. Whether we blame our brains or the Speechless Real, until now unaware of the Riddle and the Trick, and, indeed, of our Supreme Sense, we have meekly accepted the cost of not understanding Nature's Protections. Our brains tell us that despite feeling ill at ease in our nature, such is life, this is how we are meant to be, there is nothing we can do.

But this is wrong, because in our ignorance of the human condition we have resigned ourselves to a permanent state of imperfection, our potential forever beyond our reach. This, emphatically, is not how it is meant to be.

Let us recall that we are the first, and so far, the only species of emotional beings and, apart from the size of our brains, the things that truly distinguish us from the rest of creation are emotions and love. To borrow words from Byron, emotions and love make us the essence of the true sublime. In other words, they are the very things that make us truly human. Yet, curiously, the very things that make us truly human are those that cause us to feel ill at ease in our humanity.

This is because with one hand Nature endowed us with emotions and love, whilst, through the Riddle and the Trick, she hijacked them with the other, commandeering them for the greater protection of life. And so, Nature's Protections for Life (with a big 'L') are the source of our unease, directly affecting the way that we live life (with a small 'l'). In this manner, Nature sets the survival of our genes, meaning the preservation of Life, above the quality of the life we live.

Such is our true reality and the cause of all our troubles as emotional human beings. This line from Robert Browning's poem 'Andrea del Sarto' sums up our predicament: 'So free we seem, so fettered fast we are!'

The fact that the things that make us feel human make us uncomfortable in our humanity is not so much a paradox as is the fact that, not being aware of what Nature has done, we assume that our discomfort is part of being human. For we do consider ourselves to be free, free to live our own lives as we choose, to make our own decisions, to do as we please in every respect. And, muddling through with emotions and love we are, indeed, free in every respect – but one.

We are free, save for the impact that Nature's Protections have upon the way in which we live our lives.

What does this mean? It means that we are fettered fast. We have emotions that we can neither understand nor control, responding to the needs of our genes rather than to our own needs as we would perceive them; a capacity to love, seeming to have an agenda of its own, that we cannot explain; and an all-consuming, overriding need to be loved, a primary driving force for all Humankind, influencing all thoughts and actions, that we cannot resist.

These are the things over which we have no control. They affect us all whatever the circumstances, whatever our state of mind, causing us to feel ill at ease in our nature.

And this is the story so far. We are back, as in our opera, with a story of misunderstanding, missed opportunity and dysfunction. It is the human story.

There is absolutely nothing that we can do about it. Emotions and love serve two different masters. When the needs of our selves and of Nature are held in the balance, the needs of Nature must inevitably prevail. This is why our story has gone spectacularly wrong; yet, with Nature seeking to protect the Life we bear and Humankind passionately wanting to live it and survive, are not we and Nature really on the same side?

Which brings us to the Mystery, both simply stated and well named. It asks the obvious question. How can we ever thrive as the individual, self-contained, conscious, intelligent, emotional beings we are meant to be, when, for the better survival of our genes, our emotions (the Riddle) and our capacity to love and need to be loved (the Trick) have been usurped by Nature?

We are within sight of the answer to this question and, with it, the solution to all our problems. For the Mystery stands sentinel at the door to our Supreme Sense. Released from the Speechless Real and the consequent shackles of ignorance, we can and will thrive as emotional beings through our Supreme Sense. We will do so by means of the most unexpected interaction between our emotions and love, placing them both in an entirely new, ineffable role.

Let us quickly return to Jacques Barzun's statement in Chapter Three about the impossibility of explaining what it feels like to be alive, since it was our initial attempt to define that feeling that has brought us to our Supreme Sense. In that chapter I wrote that to define the feeling 'we must attempt the impossible. We must try to synthesise all the passions, feelings, thoughts, prayers and beliefs, all the moods, reactions and emotions which, together, make up the human experience of being alive, and see if we can extract from that a single factor that is present in them all. It is like seeking an alchemy, reducing all experience to a feeling we can describe; it is like discovering the Philosopher's Stone.' Well, in discovering our Supreme Sense we have done just that. We shall consider it in detail but let us say at once that it answers Barzun's question of what it feels like to be alive. The answer to that question lies within our Supreme Sense, our inner sense, dominant amongst all other senses, assisting us to protect the Life within us by keeping a check on our survival so that we may gauge precisely how we are surviving at all times.

To understand how it works we must go back to our emotions as protectors of our genes. As we know through the Riddle, our emotions react to every experience, responding negatively when there is a perceived threat to the needs of our genes and positively when there is a perceived opportunity to fulfil their potential.

Reacting to the needs of our genes in this way, our emotions present themselves complete and various and quite beyond our control. We have never before understood them. We do not entirely understand them yet. But we shall. To do so we have to translate their message into feelings that we can readily follow and comprehend.

Nature is concerned with survival. Our emotions are dedicated to survival. Love is proximate to survival, which is why we all need to be loved.

Now, this is crucial. In gauging how we are surviving, and how well our genes are being protected, our Supreme Sense interprets our emotions by reference to how they impact on our all-important and personal need to be loved (with 'love' defined in its extended sense). If our emotions register positively against our need to be loved, we are surviving; if they do not, we are not.

Everything that happens to us, every experience we shall ever have, is universally processed in this way, analysing our emotions by reference to their impact on our unique and very human need to be loved.

And so, we reach the absolutely fundamental question of all humanity: 'Am I loved?' It is this question that our Supreme Sense asks hundreds of times each day to check on how we are surviving, converting each emotion to something we can readily understand, each experience into feelings it can process. 'Am I loved?' Here is the language of survival, the answer being determined by reference to whether our emotions are having a positive or negative effect on our greatest need, our need to be loved.

Our lives are thus spent converting our emotional responses to human experience into feelings of being loved or not loved, thereby enabling us to ascertain how we are surviving at any one time. In this way, an emotion will make us feel loved or it will not, and consequently we will feel that we are surviving or we will not, whether or not we realise it. For love is genuinely proximate to survival and the degree to which we feel ourselves loved is the measure of our survival.

Consider what this means. We have the answer to practically every personal, psychological and emotional problem; at last we can understand ourselves and realise that despite all of our ambitions, strategies, schemes and plans, we are, in fact, motivated and driven by nothing other than our wholesome, humble need to be loved. To illustrate this, let us return one final time to Sloane Street, to find ourselves variously caught in the rain, stood up for lunch, perhaps mugged, sacked from our job or dumped by a girlfriend's text, each event construed by our emotions as a gene-threatening event. The understandable negative feelings of anger, distress, fury, insecurity engendered by these events can also be ascribed to the lack of one or more of our component emotions of love: being caught in the rain to lack of benevolence; being stood up for lunch to lack of respect, consideration or friendship; being mugged to lack of benevolence, respect or sympathy; being sacked to lack of gratitude, consideration, affection, attraction, friendship, respect or compassion; being dumped to lack of gratitude, consideration, affection, romance, desire, fondness, friendship, esteem, devotion, care or compassion.

Translated in this way into a language we can all understand, our emotions are entirely intelligible. Their language, the language of our Supreme Sense, is the language of love.

What we actually feel as we process our personal emotions is what makes each of us individually different, separate, self-aware and unique from everyone else. What we feel is what makes us human. It is the core feeling of all humanity, our essence as emotional beings. 'Am I loved?' asks our Supreme Sense, constituting the single constant in all human existence.

And the feeling thus engendered, the absolute feeling of me, the awareness of myself as a breathing, thinking human being sovereign in my body and my mind, in every respect whole and separate from every other person in the world, reacting to all stimuli and happenings, and, determined to survive, always asking 'Am I loved?' to check on the extent to which my overriding need to be loved is being fulfilled and thus how I am surviving: this and nothing else is our spectacular feeling of being alive; this and nothing else is what it feels like to be alive.

See what this means.

Our Supreme Sense is the sense that makes absolute sense of existence, resolving the profound problems arising from the Riddle and the Trick, realigning our interests with those of Nature, enabling us to function in a way that up until now we would only have dreamed of. The operation of our Supreme Sense is what it feels like to be me (or you, or her or him), a feeling that no-one else can possibly share, since all of us are individual, unique and utterly different, and the experiences, emotions, and feelings that we have are totally private to ourselves. Our life, our feeling of self, our personal awareness, our very individuality and sense of identity are brought into being by our Supreme Sense, all through the simple conversion of emotions into feelings of being loved or not loved.

This is the essence of what it is actually like to be me, of how it feels being human, experiencing my life, assessing every single situation that I am ever exposed to, making me a genuinely unique individual.

Surely we have found our humanity, the single, tender human thing that marks us off from the rest of Creation? By assessing our emotions in this way, each of us is as different to each other as are the personal experiences giving rise to our emotions, yet each of us is a whole and separate human being, a private universe completely individual and distinct from anyone else. Now we can see how Nature endowed the human condition with a spectacular faculty to know and feel ourselves as I, the only I apart from God, to know what it feels like to be me, something no-one else can possibly know.

'Am I loved?' All human sensation is experienced by the answer to that question and, as the years go by, the accumulation of answers creates an intimate register of feeling born of experience, a self, providing foundation to our character and identity.

It is no exaggeration to describe our Supreme Sense as our custodian in relation to everything we shall ever experience. For every thought, every joy, every pleasure, every setback, every danger, every challenge, every trauma, every risk, every relationship, every single thing that will ever happen to us, however dramatic, however mundane, is assessed in this way by our omnipresent, life-enhancing Supreme Sense, defining our sense of self, giving shape to our existence and, most importantly, helping us to survive.

The imbalance between ourselves and Nature as presented by Nature's Protections is no more, our imperfections have melted away, our unfathomable emotions have danced with love to a tune that we never heard before.

Here is our very spirit, our sense of soul, what others recognise in us as our essential being. Here is our elusive sentience, surely the very foundation of consciousness, propelling us far above all other creatures who have ever lived. Here is how we are intended to live, what it feels like to be alive, at last understanding the human condition, at peace with ourselves and the world we share, at ease in our being and comfortable in our nature.

But... there is always a but. If our Supreme Sense completes our understanding of the human condition, there is yet a snag. There is always a snag in life and no exception is made for our Supreme Sense.

This explains why so many people are not at ease and live unfulfilled, disappointed, unhappy lives. For the snag is not in relation to our Supreme Sense itself – which, as we have described, is all-embracing and fully effective – but in relation to ourselves. We function by reference to our Supreme Sense but have been unaware of its existence or of how it makes us as we are. And, sadly, as we intimated right at the start when we referred to the simple bit that comes at the end, the majority of us ask the wrong question. We shall see the unfortunate consequences of doing this in the next chapter.

11

'Am I Loved?' or 'Am I Surviving?', and Nature's Morality

Never, no, never, did Nature
say one thing and wisdom another
EDMUND BURKE (1729–97)

Before Man made us citizens,
great Nature made us men.
JAMES RUSSELL LOWELL (1819–91), 'On the Capture
of Certain Fugitive Slaves near Washington' (1845)

'Humility is only doubt,' wrote William Blake. But we have no doubts. What we are about to explain makes perfect, if unexpected, sense. It is the logical conclusion to all we have considered together, and, in so far as it reveals that, unaware of how Nature intended them to live, the overwhelming majority of human beings, both those alive today and all those who preceded them, have lived incomplete and sometimes unsatisfactory lives, then this chapter will explain the things they were unaware of, helping us all to find happiness, fulfilment and ease in the future by living our lives as we were always intended to do.

'Life is a maze in which we take the wrong turning before we have learned to walk.' This quotation from Cyril Connolly in *The Unquiet Grave* (1944) very neatly defines the problem. For no-one is to blame for our mistakes. They are our inheritance. An inheritance from previous generations unchallenged through the ages and never questioned until now.

Take a short look at our world, hopelessly divided as it is against itself, its inhabitants sadly too often jealous, covetous, competitive, insecure, having identified themselves in varying and often overlapping degrees, by reference to tribe, race, nation, religion, politics, ideology or economic or social status. Such is and has always been the way of human existence, our lives a miracle of order until inevitably things go wrong. We are consumed by our differences; indeed, we are sustained by them, often unsatisfied, ever striving yet often unfulfilled, and ever ignorant of the human condition, of how easy it would be to find the fulfilment we are searching for, if only we knew how.

But there is another, entirely different way to consider Humankind. Embedded in our societies as these symbols of identity may be, there is an altogether better way to classify ourselves and others. 'It is only with the heart that one can see rightly: what is essential is invisible to the eye.' These words, written by Antoine de Saint-Exupéry (*The Little Prince*) shortly before his early death in a wartime plane crash, point us in the right direction.

For we have to discuss what no-one has understood before. Human society may indeed be divided into myriad divisions and sub-divisions, but for us to understand ourselves and find fulfilment it needs only to be divided into two. Because, when it comes to the need to be loved, to the single thing that really matters to every individual above all else, Humankind has no need of further divisions.

Surprising as it may seem, none of the gradations of society that bind us together and yet keep us apart are of any possible relevance. We can abandon them all. One will do, simply dividing the whole of Humankind into those who ask one question and those who ask another. Or, put another way, into those who ask the right question and those, sadly constituting the overwhelming majority, who ask the wrong one. All other divisions are otiose and redundant.

We have reached a fork in our hitherto straight road, a bifurcation, an unexpected need for direction which sees the bulk of Humankind taking one road when it was always intended by Nature that they should take the other. Here is the great divide, the great choice, the great game changer, where it can truly be said: 'Oh ye'll tak the high road, and I'll tak the low road, and I'll be…' a vastly different person to you.

As with all travellers faced with alternative routes, we have a choice to make. The choice, initiated by our Supreme Sense, comes down to one of two questions: 'Am I loved?' or 'Am I surviving?' Strictly as a matter of logic most people assume that 'Am I surviving?' is the correct and obvious question to ask. After all, our Supreme Sense exists to check on how we are surviving and that is what we are all concerned to do. But whilst it may appear to be the correct question, we shall see that it is in fact the wrong one, as it ultimately leads to nowhere but an emotional cul-de-sac.

This requires an explanation. Having emerged from the confusion of the Speechless Real, it may us take a little while yet to escape fully from its shadow. For our new perceptions are unfamiliar and untried and our previous comfort and ignorance may not be easily disturbed. So, let us recall our journey so far.

The survival of the Life we bear is the sole rationale of all existence, it is the absolute force within Creation. Remember that Life's survival is Nature's sole reason for our being on this earth. Whether a microscopic mite, invisible to the naked eye, or a thirty-ton whale, every single Life-bearing being or thing is the same, concerned to survive through the protection of the genes that built it.

With human beings, our genes are protected by our emotions, but, as we have seen, until we had knowledge of our Supreme Sense our emotions were beyond our understanding or control. Our Supreme Sense gauges our survival by reference to the effect that our emotional responses have on our prime need to be loved.

Being loved and feeling loved is the greatest prize of our existence. It is the only way that we can satisfy our need to be happy and whole, and at one with our nature, crucially bringing added security to our genes through the loving concern of others.

Our need to be loved, our greatest need of all, therefore provides language for our Supreme Sense. Its simple vocabulary describes the extent to which our emotions make us feel loved or not loved. That is all that our Supreme Sense needs to determine how we are surviving. Does an emotional response make us feel loved or not loved? Hence, the question 'Am I loved?'

Let us apply this to our positive experiences to see how it works. We fall in love, win an Oscar, recover from cancer and suddenly our hearts are soaring, we are jumping for joy, feeling ecstatic, happy and secure. These feelings are affirmative answers to the question 'Am I loved?'

However, things can look very different with negative emotions, for two reasons. One: having been dumbed down by ignorance of the Supreme Sense since the beginning of human time, the majority within all previous generations, and indeed our own to a very large extent, have devoted their passions to personal survival using the language of survival rather than love. And two: as the function of our Supreme Sense is to gauge how we are surviving, 'Am I surviving?' may seem an obvious question to ask. After all, the notion of survival is more immediate than that of being loved, which requires giving and commitment and takes time. If someone harms me, if I am injured in an accident or the victim of hardship or distress, am I more likely to ask 'Am I loved?' or 'Am I surviving?'

But, hard as it may be to grasp, this misses the point, because if the choice of asking 'Am I surviving?' is simple and obvious, it is nevertheless made without understanding. For if I am harmed, injured or subject to hardship or distress, I am as unlikely to consider myself to be loved as I am to consider myself to be surviving. But love is about surviving and, crucially, love is the sole language of our Supreme Sense. It has no other. Needing to be loved is our greatest need, therefore being loved is the reality of survival. Concentrating on survival itself to the exclusion of love is not only to use the wrong language but to traduce our very need to be loved (which encompasses our need to survive as part of itself and is the direct route to fulfilment and ultimate ease in ourselves).

As for our ancestors, so for ourselves. The consequences of asking the wrong question are far-reaching, affecting the very fabric of our lives. Survival becomes an end in itself. For the majority of people it becomes the be-all and end-all of existence, giving rise to an excessive determination to survive in social, material, economic and financial terms. Survival is placed ahead of all relationships and all other considerations, influences and virtues.

Of course, there are two kinds of survival: survival defined in economic, material or social terms, and survival as robust, intact, loving human beings fulfilled in themselves and their humanity. As we can see, these are entirely different things. Consider:

- 'Am I loved?' is giving.
- 'Am I surviving?' is taking.
- 'Am I loved?' is being lovable and loving others.
- 'Am I surviving?' is loving oneself.
- 'Am I loved?' brings solutions.
- 'Am I surviving?' brings problems.

Look closer at modern life, at the dead eyes, the blank stares, the ruthless ambition of individuals concerned only for themselves, at the broken or semi-detached relationships, the abused spouses and partners, the damaged children, at the unloving, self-obsessed individuals careless of the feelings of others, indeed of anything that does not appear to advance their personal survival as they see it, and you will appreciate the consequences of only asking 'Am I surviving?'

Without the former props of family and religion, and with more and more people choosing to live alone, surviving has become more hazardous. People do not commit fully to relationships; manners and courtesies, the lubricants of life, are forgone; and life is hard, lonesome and brittle. No longer is survival a physical thing, it is now about doing better than other people in what becomes a downward spiral of loveless non-fulfilment.

Without realising that there was a choice, people have been asking the wrong question. But there is an irony here, because asking 'Am I surviving?' necessarily involves the sterile state of loving oneself in place of others, whereas asking 'Am I loved?' contains the promise of loving others, being loveable and therefore loved.

We stated at the beginning of this chapter that we had no doubts. We know what is right, but is it practicable?

Life is seldom black and white, and navigating our existence is a subtle process as we are all gloriously human in its most vulnerable sense. So, let us recognise that not everyone will ask the right question all of the time. After all, all of us are fallible.

And let us also consider whether it will be realistic or fair to expect those who seldom or never ask the right question to change their ways. It is both possible and desirable to do so, for the consequences are wholly beneficial and far-reaching. It is, of course, also altruistic to do so and, therefore, in everyone's interest, as it involves no more than shifting the focus from egoism and selfishness to regard for others. At the end of the day, this can only lead to a better existence, especially as there is every incentive for us to ask the right question, since everyone desperately wants to be loved.

Asking the right question is, therefore, to everyone's advantage. So, take note that no sacrifice is required to give up the naked pursuit of survival. It involves merely swapping a negative for a positive mindset. It is no more than that, just relinquishing a bad habit, even though the prospect of doing so may initially appear daunting.

Having pronounced it the right question to ask and urged it upon you, I must clarify the meaning of 'Am I loved?' We ask it to establish the degree to which an experience satisfies our need to be loved. That great need may be satisfied or left unfulfilled to a lesser or greater extent depending upon the experience.

And so it is that the question 'Am I loved?' necessarily embraces all aspects of love as we have previously defined it. It follows, as we have already seen, that many, if not most, human problems can probably be reduced to feelings of not being loved, with the result that an increasing number of human difficulties can become potentially solvable. Suddenly, life will appear simpler, less complicated, less combative and fraught, once it is realised that the great unifier of all humanity, however powerful or poor, is the basic but all-important need to be loved and that all human problems generally stem from the fact that an individual in a particular context does not feel himself or herself to be loved.

Where does this leave us? Potentially, temptingly so, feeling more at ease in our nature, in reach of an enhanced existence and greater fulfilment, and with a much simpler path for experts to negotiate when mending broken hearts and spirits.

Which brings us to Nature's role in all this, to the final topping on the human condition, its crown. Though not essential to our functioning as human beings, the balancing between ourselves and Nature creates a harmony which has not been recognised before. Tennyson described Nature as 'red in tooth and claw'; that is how she has always been regarded in the animal world. But, in the context we are now considering, it can be forgotten, with the introduction of the term 'Nature's Morality' – and, no, it is not an oxymoron. It represents our ultimate level of inter-dependence, taking human existence to the highest level. Nature's Morality is how things should work but, due to human nature and human ignorance, it is not particularly how they have worked in the past.

Now that we understand the human condition and the relevance of the question 'Am I loved?', the concept comes into its own. It is the icing on the human cake, the route to the greatest happiness and fulfilment, the culmination of all we have considered, but it is also a device contrived by Nature, another exercise in psychology to obtain the ends she is seeking.

It all comes back to Nature's concern to protect the Life within us, our need to be loved as interpreted by our Supreme Sense and the question 'Am I loved?' If the answer is 'Yes', then Nature's Morality kicks in. For the concept works only when people feel themselves loved, providing each other and the Life we carry with a greater degree of protection in the form of an extra pair of eyes, ears and hands, and a general concern for those we love and who love us in return. Furthermore, through the Trick, this translates into a greater likelihood that our genes will pass down to the next generation.

Here is the ultimate perfection of Nature's gifts to us, to help us to protect the Life we bear.

How does it work? Nature's Morality is the personification of altruism. If we feel ourselves loved we must be lovable, behaving lovingly in a manner considerate of the person who loves us. If A loves B and B loves A then a compact exists for mutual concern and protection.

Extend this through a network of loving relationships, through families, between the generations, through friends and, applying the extended definition of love, through acquaintances, and you will see that a network is quickly created not just for the wellbeing of us all as individuals, but to ensure that the Life we bear is better protected for Nature.

It is not only in our very best interest to live our lives in this way, but very much to our advantage to do so. The result, that individuals at large behave lovingly (in its extended definition) whether in a loving relationship or not, and with consideration for each other, represents an expanding inter-dependence between individuals and Nature, whilst Nature also achieves a network to ensure the better protection of Life.

Love begets love. Act lovingly and receive love in return. Give love and feel loved, feel loved and feel complete, fulfilled, protected and happy. Just as to have a friend you must be a friend, it follows that to have respect you must give respect, to be esteemed you must esteem others, to be valued you must value others as well. Life is thus lived on a higher plane.

Nature's Morality is born of Nature's concern to preserve the Life within us. It may appear to be foreign to human nature to behave in this way, as it is not the way of most people; it may bear the hallmarks of religious perception, as it is moral and good, requiring a standard of conduct that we are not generally equipped to live up to; it may constitute a way of giving that we reserve only for the few people we truly love, as it calls for a similar degree of giving to ourselves; but it is manifestly in our best interests to uphold it. And then, behold, the results!

Living according to Nature's Morality affords the soundest way possible for us to feel happiness and fulfilment on this troubled planet. And it all stems from the operation of our Supreme Sense and the question 'Am I loved?'

This works with or without a belief in God. But asking 'Am I loved?' eventually leads to a win–win situation. If the answer is 'Yes', we already know that loving is giving, and giving to others rather than to ourselves is likely to help us to feel loved. On the other hand, if the answer is 'No', at least we can process the problem according to Nature's Morality, by trying to understand what has caused our negative responses and thus, why we are upset. It may not make the hurt go away but at least it will put it in its true perspective, for at the root of every problem is the non-fulfilment of someone's need to be loved, whether it be ours or somebody else's. We cannot always feel loved and indeed, sometimes, our hurt will have nothing to do with another person or a person we love, but at least we can always remember that feeling loved is what we most need.

It may seem that we are describing a new form of Godless religion, one based on self-interest yet altruistic, moral and good. But this is Nature's Morality, not God's. It is concerned with love, not obedience, with love as the ultimate currency, the ultimate incentive for us to conduct our lives in a manner calculated to fulfil our need to be loved. For love is a construct of Nature, evolved especially for us to protect the Life within us as human beings.

And so, with it being very much in our best personal interests to live according to Nature's Morality, we have discovered a new way of living. As moral as religion yet without religion, providing all that we may have dreamed of having in the next world, yet in this one, without dogma, sanctimony or self-righteousness. But, be assured that it is entirely compatible with a continuing, indeed a fervent, faith in God. Nature's Morality is a way of living with or without a personal belief in God and one that most religions would uphold.

We have now come full circle. Having eradicated the Speechless Real and found our Supreme Sense, we can at last see that we never before understood Nature properly. She may not care for us as individuals but Nature has gone to extraordinary lengths to protect the Life that we bear within us, primarily by giving us emotions and the need to be loved. Through our Supreme Sense, these have served to make us into sensitive, self-aware human beings, all of whom depend upon love for our internal stability, happiness and fulfilment.

Remember this: the bogies that caused people to conjure up a belief in the next world have been laid to rest. The things that we did not understand about ourselves in this world we do now understand, and we realise that Nature was always on our side, that our interests in being loved and in survival went hand in hand, that it is not necessary to wait for all that we desire for ourselves until the next world, as it is easily available to us now.

Such is Nature's Morality.

But back to the two questions. This book is nothing if not about human nature, so we can but point out the advantages of asking the correct question and observe that by always or often asking the wrong one, we are destined merely to end up in a vicious circle of repeating all the negative emotions that cause us distress. So, 'Am I loved?' is the question to ask; according to Nature's Morality this is the way to conduct ourselves; the Supreme Sense is what makes us individual, self-aware human beings.

Finally, here is a diagram to illustrate what we have discussed about our two questions. The first illustrates the consequences of asking 'Am I loved?' The second is based on the question 'Am I surviving?' The first is a template for a happy life. The second leads nowhere.

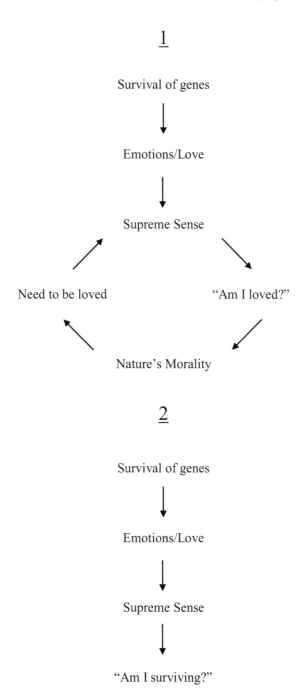

12

Oh My God

*Man is quite insane. He wouldn't know how to
create a maggot, and he creates gods by the dozen.*
MICHEL DE MONTAIGNE (1533–92)

*It doesn't matter. Tell Him that. The more cause
He gives to doubt him. Tell Him that. The deeper
delves faith. Though his love becomes only abrasion,
derision, excoriation, tell Him, I cling. He made us,
He can never shake us off. We will always find Him
out. Promise Him that. We will always find Him,
no matter how few there are, tell Him we will find
Him to deliver our complaint.*
S. ANSKY (1863–1920) *A Dybbuk* (1920)

In 1956 'In God we Trust' became the motto of the
United States of America. It appears on the bank notes
and coins of the mighty US dollar.

God is the King, not just of the Earth but of the Universe,
which is so vast that were it reduced to the size of the Earth our
world would be no bigger than the microscopic single-celled

organism that was the first bearer of Life; so vast that news of the first Cro-Magnon men and women, from 35,000 years ago, even if travelling at the speed of light, would have made it just a third of the way across our galaxy, whilst news of God would have travelled only a tenth of that distance, 3,500 light years, and that of Jesus a mere 2,000 light years.

God's presence is ubiquitous. The bulk of humanity has a relationship with him. In old age, Robert Frost in 'Cluster of Faith' wrote:

> Forgive, O Lord, my little jokes on Thee,
> And I'll forgive Thy great big one on me.

One of the themes of this book has been our general ignorance of the human condition. Likewise, Humankind has ever been ignorant of the reality of God and many of the laws of Nature. These three things can be represented within the word 'ignorance' itself, as it starts with an I for 'I', followed by a G for 'God' and an N for 'Nature'. Between them, they have been responsible for a very great deal of confusion.

> Dear God, please don't let my baby die…
> Our Father, which art in Heaven…
> I'm begging you, Lord, she's just a little baby. Please help me.
> Hear, O Israel, the Lord our God, the Lord is One…
> Don't take my baby from me. I feel so helpless, she's going to die.
> Hail Mary, full of grace…
> Dear Lord, I promise, I'll never ask for anything again.

May His great name be exalted and sanctified in this world
    which He created…
Heavenly Father, she's a baby, she's never done any harm.
Have mercy, Lord, save us, we beseech thee…
I'll do anything, anything you say, just don't let my baby
    die, I beg you.
I believe in one God, the Father Almighty…
I can't believe it, please, Lord, please, I'm begging you.
The blessings of God Almighty, the Father, the Son…
Listen to me, God, LISTEN TO ME!

If each prayer addressed in any one of the 6,000 or so languages by any one of the seven-billion-plus people in the world today, to any of the invisible gods of our invisible faiths, were an individual source of food, then together they would eradicate hunger. For, day and night, rising over the rooftops, power lines and trees, above the public squares and market places, the traffic jams, farms and wooded hills, ever upwards into the vast and empty skies, the prayers of Humankind constantly speak to God, pleading, in the often quoted words of Ambrose Bierce, 'that the laws of the universe be annulled on behalf of a single petitioner confessedly unworthy'.

Religion, or the belief in or worship of God, plays a massive role in the human drama. As Voltaire observed, 'If God did not exist it would be necessary to invent him.' And, perhaps, we have done just that, inventing and reinventing him again and again to satisfy our hunger for a supreme being, a super-supra-man to believe in, an all-powerful, omniscient Creator, Father and King, someone who cares for us, an unseen, all-seeing God to guide us, the original Holy Being who, in exchange for faith, love and obedience, grants us everlasting love.

God is a mystery we can never fully comprehend, a sublime, ineffable mystery that becomes more mysterious the more we try to understand it. And being a mystery is God's ultimate appeal.

Writing in *The English Constitution* (1867), Walter Bagehot said of the British royal family: 'Its mystery is its life. We must not let the daylight upon it.' Such, too, is God's mystery. But God's mystery is an unalterable fact, not an artifice, a fact we can never properly imagine or describe, as it comprises things of which we know nothing at all.

God's true nature remains beyond our understanding. We cannot conceive of who or what he is, the power he wields, the extent of his universe, how he came into being, what was before the universe, what may exist beyond it. All we know for sure is that God is a mystery in relation to which all interpretations are possible. Denied full knowledge of him, we can choose only to believe in him or to reject him. But such is God's influence that even those who reject him define themselves by reference to their rejection, so that as non-believers they are known as, and call themselves, atheists.

Those who believe in God have faith in a mystery, setting his competence at whatever level they may elect. And this has led to the creation of no fewer than three monotheistic religions, each with their own customs and beliefs in God, each worshipping him according to different rules, rituals and texts, with the faithful of each prepared to lay down their lives in defence of their beliefs, based, as we have said, on their faith in a mystery.

Beginning with Mount Sinai as recently as 3,500 years ago, we have lived through the daily rhythms of our lives performing God's rituals, obeying his laws, praising and glorifying him, even as we have gone to war in his name; our most fundamental assumptions, traditions, cultures and beliefs have been fashioned after his image; almost every aspect of our lives, including a good deal of art and vocabulary and many of our greetings, have evolved as a result of our faith in him.

And yet 'I know thee not, old man'. God exists as a matter of faith, not fact, as a mystery, a slice of magic upon an angel's wing, but he exists because we want him to exist. He exists because we need him to exist. He exists because the very law of Nature appointing our great need to be loved as a yardstick for survival has planted within each and every one of us a yearning, all but insatiable, need to be loved by a god, and that need, our need, has attached itself to him.

Imagine, in this sceptical age of ours, if popes spoke as presidents: 'Ask not if God exists; deliver the proof that he does.' Some challenge. Some question, never asked of us before. What need of mystery, what need of faith, if it could be proved that God exists?

Would it be like the coming of the Messiah, or the Second Coming, would the dead rise up, would there be bliss and paradise on earth?

No. All hell would break loose. There would be turmoil, there would be chaos and broken promises and broken dreams. There would be riots and wars and general heartbreak. For

God would not turn out to be anything like the God we have prayed to and imagine him to be.

A human thread runs through our God as if he were made in our image rather than we in his. We have invested our love in him, expecting him to respond as we would respond to the love and devotion we have invested in him. Such is the mindset of believers, identifying God's protection with our survival.

But let us be warned: whatever has been our understanding of him according to the conflicted teaching and beliefs of the three great monotheistic religions would no longer be sustainable. Much of what we believed would be shown to have been wrong, along, no doubt, with the world's other religions.

What would this do to the believers, to the billions of individuals who see, understand and love God in their own personalised, comfortable and possibly eccentric way? What would it do to the remaining billions, those who do not believe in God at all, if they were suddenly to be confronted with the proven existence of an actual all-seeing, omnipotent God?

What kind of character would God be revealed as having? Would he have the fierce and intemperate emotions that he is painted with in the Old Testament (a God that Harold Bloom describes in *The Book of J* as 'behav[ing] sometimes as though he is rebelling against his Jewish mother') or the gentler, more forgiving personality suggested by the teachings of the New Testament?

Conversely, what if we could prove that God does not exist at all? What then for the believers? What then for the concept of immortality, the notion of the next world, the sanctity of life? What then for the restraints and morality and self-control of God's many laws and rules? What then for judgment for our sins, the rewards of Heaven and the damnation of Hell? What then for the angels and prophets, the Messiah, the Son of God? What then for the love we give to God so freely and the blessings, care and love we believe we receive in return? What then for those who do believe and will find it impossible to stop believing? What then for the feeling that we are all absolutely on our own, unprotected and adrift on a Godless planet, unknown and invisible in the great universe around us? What then the purpose of life? What then for the comfort of believing in an omniscient Father and King who hears our prayers, reads our thoughts and knows all that is going to happen to us? What then for our prayers and traditions, the dogmas, rituals and rites of passage, the deep comforts of religion, the feeling of identity and belonging? What then for our holy books and teachings? What then for our festivals and our history? What then for our personal feelings as practising Christians, Jews, Muslims, Hindus and Buddhists? What then? What then to take the place of God, to regulate our lives, care for us and our families, bless us all and reward us for our piety and devotion? What then for all that has been done in God's name, both the good and the bad? What then for the priests, the rabbis, imams and monks, the churches and cathedrals, the synagogues, mosques and temples, the customs and traditions that have regulated our lives for generations? What then for the institutions of religion that order and protect society? What then for Faith, what then for Hope, what then for Charity?

What then our future? What then do we put in God's place?

I have asked these questions, but, fascinating as they may be, they are not for us to respond to here. Let us not debate the existence of God; rather, let us cut through the mystery of God, to examine why it is that Humankind has chosen to worship God and conduct its existence subject to his authority.

Why do a majority of the world's population believe in an invisible God who listens to our prayers and reads our thoughts, yet already knows what is going to happen to us in the future? If he were introduced to us now, without our prior belief in primitive gods, in the deities of the Greeks and the Romans and, finally, in him, the God of Abraham, would we still embrace him as our Father and Supreme King of Kings?

Yes, probably we would. For whilst there is no such thing as a 'God gene' to bring us to him, there is, and always has been within us, a yearning desire for God. But why?

There are several reasons why we are drawn to a higher being, all born of our own discomfort. Our lives on earth are plagued by insecurities and uncertainties, made worse by the Speechless Real. We don't understand the life within us, where it has come from, what will happen to us when we die. In our ignorance we do not see the purpose of life, especially because, as emotional beings, we are rendered vulnerable and ill at ease by not understanding or controlling our emotions. We have an overriding need to be loved which is all too often left unfulfilled. We are born only to die.

Out of this confusion the allure of God is seductive. Because believing in God means looking for God to love and care for us. Here is a promise of our ultimate survival. Believing that we are receiving God's blessings and protection satisfies our immediate need to be loved. Believing that we are both surviving and receiving his love fortifies our faith.

Survival, love and faith, therefore, constitute our passage to God. Positive though these concepts are, each of them emerges from negative elements in our make-up. Thus, lack of ease in our nature spurs on our desire for survival; our sense of fear of this world and, indeed, of God, encourages our search for love; our ignorance of the human condition inspires our quest for faith.

In biblical language, our negatives beget our positives, our imperfections and inadequacies beget the sublime. Put plainly, what makes us uncomfortable in ourselves causes us to look beyond our earthly lives to a higher existence.

Thus have we found God, Heaven and Hell. Thus have we founded the three great monotheistic religions.

We must look at this clearly. We have used the terms 'survival', 'love' and 'faith' to describe our road map to God. But, whatever words we use, the end result we are looking for is, once again, survival. For, in the end, we believe in God for one overwhelming and practical reason, more tangible than faith and more urgent than devotion. However we may construe our love for him, our belief in God is determined by just a single need, one we share with all creation although the rest of creation knows him not: our ever-present and all-powerful need for survival.

13

For God's Sake

Ignorance of Nature gave birth to Gods. Then knowledge of Nature is destined to destroy them.
PAUL-HENRI THIRY, BARON D'HOLBACH (1723–89)
La Système de la nature (1770)

A person can't love God because one can't see God and He's almighty and eternal. How can a person conduct a love affair with the sun? It's like a microbe trying to have a love affair with an elephant, but on a scale a thousand times greater.
ISAAC BASHEVIS SINGER (1902–91)
Shadows on the Hudson (1957)

Tell proud Jove
Between his power and thine there is no odds;
'Twas only fear first in the world made God.
BEN JONSON (1573–1637) *Sejanus His Fall* (1603)

Our search for survival is inspired, very largely, by fear, the apprehension of imminent danger. Fear is the great magician who caused our ancestors to conjure up gods to fix the weather, cure disease, assist hunters, bring victory; in short, to prevail against the odds to help them to survive.

Fear was a constant shadow to life when, like animals, hardly anyone died from natural causes, and most were dead by the end of their twenties. People were driven to placate their gods with sacrifice, offerings and rituals of a kind that would crush the sensibilities of today's believers. So, gods came at a price. The cost of finding them brought a whole new range of fears: of rejection, of punishment and damnation for sins of transgressing the god's laws or wishes. And, even today, having humanised God, part of our relationship with him involves fear, as many believers consciously live their entire lives in fear of going to Hell or missing out on paradise.

Along with fear, a negative emotion whose function is to help us to survive, comes faith and love, two positive emotions very much intended to help us to thrive.

It is these positive emotions that bring us to God, with faith conveying us and love committing us to him, to secure our survival. But the survival we are after is not quite as straightforward as physical survival in our world. It is sought through the beneficence of God and extends beyond this world and into the next.

So, how do we do it? What is faith?

Analysing something as intangible as faith is always going to be difficult. It is a buoyant, often joyous, kind of optimism that lifts us out of the miseries of human existence and takes us to God.

By definition, as faith cannot extend to an object susceptible to intellectual proof and the existence of God cannot be proved or disproved, faith becomes the capacity to believe the unbelievable. That is why we talk of believing in God. Faith is always a subjective experience, a personal experience encapsulating a private belief. This is where God will be found, not at the altar, or in the Ark, but suspended in the hearts and minds of the faithful (those full of faith), each with his or her own individual image of the God they worship.

Perhaps that is why there is today an altogether less passionate form of faith, of the kind probably held by a majority of the faithful. In our increasingly secular age, there are many people who perhaps pay lip-service to the worship of God rather than enter into their faith wholeheartedly. Rather than abandoning their faith in God entirely, such people believe in believing. And believing in believing becomes the extent and limit of their faith.

Fear, of yet a different hue, now makes its appearance. For, instead of breaking with a religion that they are conscious of believing in less and less, those who believe in believing are influenced by a fear of burning the bridges inherited from parents and ancestors or built when their faith was stronger. For them, and their numbers are probably very substantial, it is like the answer to the question addressed to Mrs Wesley: 'Why do you waste your time repeating everything to your children a hundred times?' To which she replied: 'Because I don't want to waste the other ninety nine.'

Which brings us to love and the first fault line in human reasoning about God. Consider these words from Dostoevsky, written in the year before his death: 'If you were to destroy in mankind the belief in immortality, not only love but every living force maintaining the life of the world would at once be dried up.' There could be no clearer example of how, in believing in God as a means to survival, survival depends upon faith and faith upon love. If fear is the parent of faith, then love is faith's mistress. For it is no less than love, the gauging and supplying of another's needs, that is the ultimate tool of survival on this earth, and it is love, in a trinity of faith and fear, that binds us so solidly to the idea of God.

In many ways our relationship with God is the definitive proof, if proof still be needed, of our great need to be loved. But love was given to Humankind to help protect the Life we bear on this earth. It was given to us to share with our fellow human beings, each of whom is equipped to give us love in return, thus adding an extra level of care to our prospects of survival. Remember the Trick. Love is designed to be requited, not given away without prospect of the recipient loving us back. We can love a tree, a full moon or a car but we don't expect our love to be reciprocated, but, if we love our spouse or child or friend, the chances are overwhelmingly that we do.

In our religions God exists to care for us and save us and in giving him our love we look to him to love us in return. Except, of course, he does not, or cannot, love us in any tangible sense, because the love of God cannot be requited in terms of the fulfilment of our human needs to survive or to procreate, as love on earth is specifically designed to do. 'Who so truly loves God must not expect God to love him in return,' wrote the great Spinoza, his words being applauded generations later by

Goethe, as expressing exactly his own belief. But we do expect God to love us in return, although, in the Old Testament, God never promised to do so, he only commanded us to give our love to him.

How could we not expect God to love us in return, for our faith and devotion and adherence to his rituals and laws? And, how could any human being, engineered to seek requital for loving on this earth, be expected to love without the prospect of even the faintest chance of it? To do so would be like loving a tree. All fine but strictly on a one-way basis, understanding that nothing will be received in return.

Nevertheless, we give our love, the greatest thing we are able to bestow on each other, to God. We do so obviously in the general belief that he will bless us and help us to survive, and because of a specific belief, for which there is no evidence, that our love will be requited, if not in this world then in the next, a world we shall enter after death.

And so, desperate to survive in this world and find salvation in the next, we give our love to God, submitting our fragile, individual destinies into his metaphorical hands, with a fervour and commitment which, if devoted to our fellow human beings, would, at the very least, ensure a reasonable certainty that our love would be requited in this world, perhaps many times over.

Without seeking to undermine anyone's faith, we may conjecture that in the fulfilment of Nature's Morality, if we gave the same dedication and service to Humankind as we give to God, relationships would flourish, hearts would soften, misery and suffering would be eased and the continuing resort to violence and abomination in God's name might cease altogether.

It all boils down to one simple fact. We have given to God something it was intended we should give to each other.

But back to Spinoza. In 1656, at the age of only twenty three, Spinoza was excommunicated from his community in Amsterdam, subject to an anathema whose curses, if read today, would still send a chill down the reader's spine. Notwithstanding this, he developed into one of the world's most enduring philosophers. His offence was to suggest that God and Nature might be one and the same. Remember this as we continue.

In the entire universe, comprising billions of galaxies with billions upon billions of stars extending in all directions for an unimaginable fifteen billion light years, it is just possible that we are the only beings who are aware of God's existence, let alone the only beings to worship him. If we are indeed the only beings in the universe to worship God, how ridiculous – no, how farcical – that we should do so in competing ways. Because, whatever the differences in the ways we go about it, we are all the same in merely seeking survival.

This explains the atheist zeal as much as the orthodoxies of religion or the extremes of fundamentalism. Survival is the spur to practically all human activity, whether it involves taking communion, falling in love or buying a bigger car than your neighbour. But true though this is, too often the action taken or thoughts concluded to help us to survive are based on ignorance and, strange as it may seem, it is ignorance of the human condition that is directly responsible for the three great monotheistic religions.

How can this be? We have already seen that our ignorance of the human condition and our consequent feeling of being ill at ease in ourselves have caused us to look outside our earthly existence for God. Well, here comes the second fault line in our reasoning.

'I am that I am,' said God in the Old Testament, which introduced him to the world. And we are what we are, whether or not we like it or understand it. We are no different from the children of Israel for whom the Old Testament was written, roughly three and a half billion years after the first manifestations of life but more or less as soon as there was language to express it, writing to record it and people smart enough to comprehend it.

And yet, it offers no explanation for the creation of the Life within those who would read it, the most sublime of all creations, the creations you would imagine, if any, were divine. Neither does the Bible disclose any insight into the emotional make-up of the people it was written for.

In short, God gave us rules to live by, but never explained the rules of Nature by which we live. Instead, the Old Testament exhorts us to love God rather than each other, ignoring the miracle of Life animating each being, and makes no attempt to address the emotional needs of humanity, a consequence of how Nature provided for the protection of Life. The Old Testament's portrait of an omnipresent, demanding, vengeful and jealous God has served to exploit our ignorance by increasing human insecurity and a consequent dependence upon God, whereas an explanation of those things we do not understand might have served as a balm on troubled spirits, perhaps even encouraging the proverbial lion to lie down with the proverbial lamb. The result is truly paradoxical, for we have turned to God precisely because we are ignorant, vulnerable, lacking in ease and unsure of ourselves, hailing him and depending upon him as the ultimate source of hope and salvation.

Such is the genesis of our belief in God, a belief taken up by three religions whose bitter rivalries and conflicts have perversely served to increase faith and devotion.

But there is a further irony here. Our emotions have a major role in the human condition. Being unable either to understand or control them is part of the ignorance which has caused our unease and brought us to God. And yet, the very same emotions and emotional needs have affected our daily lives more directly and more profoundly than all God's laws in the Bible.

'So God created man in his own image, in the image of God created he him' (Genesis 1.27). Of course, this verse has connotations beyond the literal relating to humanity's spirituality and, yet, looking at the character of God as it emerges from the Old Testament, we must ask again if perhaps God is made in our image rather than us in his. The reason for this is because, as intimated at the beginning of this chapter, he is revealed as emotional, almost the victim of a huge range of emotions throughout the Bible's narrative. Emotions which are immediately recognisable as identical to our own, making him, in Harold Bloom's words, 'human – all – too – human'.

We must now introduce the third and final fault line in human reasoning about God. It is inconceivable that God would have any need of emotions, or take on the mantle of human frailty by assuming an emotional character. He is, after all, the Supreme King of Kings and Lord of the Universe, the Creator of all living things. So, why would he need to have emotions when, as we have seen, emotions exist merely to protect our genes and therefore the Life within us? We would not expect Nature to have emotions, so why would God?

We are making a very serious point, because if God does not have emotions, then how can he love us? And if God does not love us, why should he listen to our prayers? And if he does not listen to our prayers, does he care for us as individual souls, or judge us? And if he does not care for us or judge us, why should there be an afterlife or a Heaven and a Hell? Indeed, does that mean that we do not have immortal souls?

If God exists but neither loves nor listens to us, nor even cares about us, then what has been the point of our religions, rituals, traditions and beliefs, and all the torments, sufferings, barbarity and death that have characterised belief in him? Why should young people blow themselves up to murder others? Why should men and women renounce a full life on this earth to devote their existence to prayer? Why should intelligent people in the twenty first century dress in the fur-hatted style of sixteenth-century Poles?

Perhaps Spinoza was right and God and Nature are indeed the

same, a single entity. If this be so, then no-one would want to go to war for God again, yet God would remain just as ineffable and all-powerful and wonderful as before, just not as human.

Before we close this chapter let us turn to something lighter. A little more confusion. A thought to amuse atheist authors whose writings seem to have overlooked a mischievous and brilliant book called *The Book of J.*

Conditioned by our cultural beliefs, we have been brought up on the stories of Creation, of Abraham, Isaac and Jacob, of Joseph and Moses, and to believe them to be sacred texts, holy sources forming the very basis of faith for the children of Abraham, the followers of Judaism, Christianity and Islam. Yet, according to Harold Bloom, justly the most distinguished of literary scholars, writing in *The Book of J*, the author of these stories is probably not Moses at the dictation of God, but someone living three or so centuries later. Moreover, the author, probably a woman known as J, composed these stories not as a religious text but as a classic literary work whose hero is neither Abraham, nor Isaac, nor Jacob, nor Joseph, nor Moses, but God himself.

As Bloom says, if this is correct, we may have been worshipping the equivalent of Hamlet all these years, looking to a literary hero to bless us and protect us and help us to survive; to regulate the lives of believers from birth to grave; to wage war, massacre and persecute; but, even more than this, if it is true, our love for God, the mainstay of faith, observance and ritual, will prove to have been a pointless, superfluous love.

Let us conclude with a short extract from the text of *The Book of J*, sensitively translated from the original Hebrew by David Rosenberg. Here is the Temptation of Eve, corresponding to Chapter 3, verses 10–17, of the book of Genesis:

> Now the snake was smoother tongued than any wild creature that Yahweh made. 'Did God really mean,' he said to the woman, 'you can't eat from any tree in the garden?'
>
> 'But the fruit of the trees we may,' said the woman to the snake. 'Just the tree in the middle of the garden, the God said. You can't eat it, you can't touch – without death touching you.'
>
> 'Death will not touch you,' said the snake to the woman. 'The God knows on the day you eat from it your eyes will fall open like gods knowing good and bad.'

Who could have resisted temptation such as that?

Perhaps, by now, our eyes have fallen open as well, just a little.

14

Humankind

We're all of us guinea pigs in the laboratory of God.
Humanity is just a work in progress.
TENNESSEE WILLIAMS (1911–83) *Camino Real* (1953)

O, wonder!
How many goodly creatures are there here!
How beauteous mankind is! O brave new world,
That has such people in't!
WILLIAM SHAKESPEARE (1564–1616)
The Tempest (c. 1610), Act 5, Scene 1

We know we are special. It took no less than three and a half billion years for us to evolve. Three and a half billion years of extraordinary and primitive, short-lived incarnations, before it was possible for us to evolve as the first, and so far the only, emotional beings.

After all that time we emerged able to subdue and dominate the world, quickly covering it in tarmac and concrete and even colonising the skies, and yet, even then, we turned out to be flawed. In fact, pitifully vulnerable to the Protections put in place by Nature to preserve the Life we bear, we emerged as the first, and so far the only, truly dysfunctional species.

There is no other way to describe us. For how else can we characterise a world whose population is

- universally ill at ease in its nature
- ignorant of its own make-up
- the hapless victims of its emotions
- conflicted by Nature's Protections
- unable to explain the feeling of being alive
- believing this is how things are meant to be, that nothing is amiss?

We are reminded of the words of Hilaire Belloc, in his *Cautionary Tales* (1907):

Physicians of the Utmost Fame
Were called at once; but when they came
They answered, as they took their Fees,
'There is no cure for this Disease...'

But we have cured the disease.

- The Speechless Real, which blanketed out all understanding of the human condition, is no more.
- We have discovered the secret of Life.
- We have resolved the Riddle.
- We have revealed the Trick.
- We have solved the Mystery.
- We now understand our emotions and are better able to deal with them.

- We have found our Supreme Sense, the source of our self-awareness and consciousness.
- We have discovered how the impact of our emotions on our need to be loved enables us, by dint of a simple question, to gauge how we are surviving.
- We have learned that asking 'Am I loved?' instead of 'Am I surviving?' is the way to happiness and fulfilment.
- We have seen how this opens the door to Nature's Morality and the promise of a loving existence incorporating into this life all that we may wish for ourselves in the next.
- We have the promise of being easily able to resolve most emotional problems in the future.

In the result we have at last

- overcome our ignorance
- understood the human condition for the first time
- taken charge of our emotions
- gained the chance to feel comfortable within ourselves and at ease in our nature.

With words more reminiscent of the yet to be born Woody Allen than of the father of psychoanalysis, Sigmund Freud stated that the goal of psychotherapy was 'to transfer hysterical misery into common unhappiness'. Well, we can do better than that.

Let us take a look at grief. Steven Pinker writes in *How the Mind Works* that 'No-one knows what, if anything, grief is for.

Obviously the loss of a loved one is unpleasant, but why should it be devastating? Why the debilitating pain that stops people from eating, sleeping, resisting disease, and getting on with life?' Grief is a perfectly legitimate emotion. Books are written about how to deal with it, how it involves passing through seven stages. But grief is not some kind of disposition that falls on the bereaved. It is far less complicated than that, having as its cause the tragic and much-regretted loss of a source of love.

As we have repeatedly stated, everybody aspires to be loved, and being loved is our very greatest need. So, on losing a source of committed love, is not grief a perfectly understandable reaction to that loss and the resultant hole in our personal make-up that only the passing of time will assuage?

If this is correct then we can go further. Consider our Supreme Sense. As our grief impacts on our need to be loved, whichever question we ask, 'Am I surviving?' or 'Am I loved?', the answer will be 'No, I am not. I am overwhelmed by my loss.' Such is grief and the reason we suffer from it.

Now apply this to psychoanalysis and, indeed, to all psychotherapies and you will find at the root of all distress, or 'hysterical misery' as Freud puts it, a feeling in the patient akin to grief, of a loss of love, as we have defined it. Somewhere, somehow, something – an event, an exchange, a happening – will have caused the patient's Supreme Sense to register that he or she is not surviving. The love that the patient had counted on and felt was theirs has not been given them or has been taken away.

In Supreme Sense terms they do not feel themselves loved, they are therefore not surviving. Hence their feelings of being depressed, diminished, angry, insecure, undermined, grief-struck, overwhelmed by despair, confused, humiliated, insulted, let down, for which they sensibly seek help.

Psychoanalysis and psychotherapies exist both to identify the cause of distress and to help the patient deal, or come to terms, with it. But, crucially, in Nature there are neither rewards nor punishments, just consequences. And practically all human problems are the consequence of a loss of love in its enlarged sense, which is very similar to the concept of grief. Understanding this should help us to see life in a more accessible perspective and speed up both the identification of our problems and, most importantly, their eventual solution.

And there is a logic to all this. Let us not forget our genes. We have previously termed them faithful rather than selfish because they exist to bring Life to us as Nature wants them to do. In turn, our emotions exist to protect them. Our survival, and through that our genes' survival, is then gauged by the impact that our emotions have on our need to be loved. This is determined by our Supreme Sense. If we do not feel ourselves loved, we are not surviving and our genes are put at risk. Such is the consequence of losing a source of love.

Love is the measure of our survival. Its loss, whether through death or any other event, is the root cause of our feeling that we are not surviving. As such, its loss is the cause both of hysterical misery and of common unhappiness.

But there is more. Although we could and probably

should engage at greater length, let us very briefly consider a fascinating question which says a great deal about Humankind and survival: of the wheel, the kiss and God (on the basis that Humankind found God in the first place), which is the greatest human invention?

Each makes a fundamental contribution to human existence, and each is unique and utterly irreplaceable in terms of its effect on our daily lives. So we will look at each individually, concerned at how we shall ever find the correct answer to the question, lest in anointing one we may by inference be deemed to be downgrading the remaining two, which it is not our intention to do.

The wheel represents the material world in which we all live and aspire to thrive. Apart from the Incas in pre-Columbian Peru, all civilisation has depended upon the wheel. Initially, it revolutionised agriculture. Since then it has been the essential building block in all developments from transport, construction, industry and technology to the most basic tools and luxuries of daily life. It is hard to imagine living without it.

In contrast, the kiss represents our emotional life. It disappears as soon as it is given. It is a messenger, not a fixture, and has no potential use. Nevertheless, given by one person to another, it is the harbinger of love, on which every generation and the future of humanity depend. It represents the very essence of what it means to be a responsive emotional human being. Life would be immeasurably poorer without it.

Finally, God represents our spiritual world. Through God we have laws and moral codes to regulate our lives and the potential to live a good and meaningful existence. Believed in as a matter of faith, we regard God as an omnipotent source of unconditional love. Notwithstanding the violence, barbarity and injustice that has been wrought and continues to be done in his name, God's contribution to humanity is unequalled and unique.

In essence, we are considering three contrasting worlds, the material, the emotional and the spiritual, and this is our clue to finding the right answer. We inhabit them all. But, as human constructs, only one is closest to Nature, directly helping Nature to achieve her desired ends.

This is the kiss. Seen from Nature's point of view, it is the only one of these inventions that makes an overwhelming contribution to her desire to protect the Life we bear. Nature has no interest in our comfort, nor in civilisation, nor even with whom we mate, nor the good or bad of religion. Her sole concern is the protection of our genes and the Life they bring. The singular gifts that she has bestowed upon us, namely our emotions and our capacity to love, come together in the kiss.

So, the kiss has it. The kiss is the greatest of these most significant of human inventions. It wins the accolade as it conforms exactly to Nature's plan for the protection of our genes, thereby immeasurably helping Humankind to survive.

The question of whether and to what extent an activity conforms to Nature's plan for the protection of our genes must be the yardstick for our final consideration of human survival. We have seen that survival is one of the most potent motivators in all aspects of human activity. If pursued the wrong way, it leads directly to Freud's hysterical misery and common unhappiness. If pursued correctly, all hope is restored.

What, therefore, is the right way?

Let me surprise you. We shall descend on the one kind of place where we are guaranteed to find extremes of human behaviour and emotions, where mistakes are made as a matter of course as people stumble to find their way, to understand how to navigate their channel through life's infinite cross-currents and changing tides, succumbing to some pressures, withstanding others, experiencing sadness, anger, insecurity and aggression, yet also finding affection, pleasure, devotion and happiness. All life is here, in this curious place where people arrive knowing next to nothing about survival and leave educated in how to survive but with very little understanding of which aspects of survival lead to love and fulfilment and which lead to a dead end.

We have all been to the place we are going to and we will all recognise it when we get there. It is a school playground and the people we are observing, whose behaviour might suggest a form of derangement if they were adult, are children learning more about life in the playground than they ever will inside the school.

Which is just as well because, despite massive strides in the development of our intellect, enabling us to create civilisation, find God and invent the internet, emotionally we have hardly developed at all since our Cro-Magnon ancestors, prior to the last Ice Age. In fact, in emotional terms, we remain in a state of adolescence where reason and stability are relegated to the rear stalls as exaggerated faults and troubles take centre stage.

In simple terms, the level of our emotional maturity has barely advanced beyond the playground, which is why we are there. But, first, let us chart the course of our children before joining the school whose playground this is, for we must have some idea of what they are like when they initially arrive.

One day, a child is in the womb and the next she is here. Sightless, speechless, entirely innocent of life and weighing less than a few cans of tuna, the child is only good for feeding, sleeping and crying. But even at this first of stages she knows exactly what she needs to survive.

'I'm wet,' 'I'm dirty,' 'I'm hungry,' 'I'm tired,' 'I'm cold,' 'I'm hot,' the child will complain, communicating through strident baby cries.

After a very short period of time the child is finding her way. 'I don't like being undressed,' 'I don't like a bath,' 'I don't want to get out of the warm water,' 'I don't want to be fussed,' 'I don't want to lie down,' 'I want to be fed,' 'I want to be snuggled,' 'I want… I want… I want…' The child is operating entirely on her emotions and, of course, as emotions do, her emotions are protecting her genes and the new Life that she bears. The child has no concerns other than for herself and her survival as an individual.

She begins to develop quickly. Soon she can see clearly, next she can smile. She is getting into a regime of feeding, sleeping and waking time. She recognises her mother. She smiles at her. Soon the same with her father. She's cute. They love her. The cuter she is, the more they smile back. This helps her get to do what she wants, when she wants to play or get up.

All the time she is surviving. That seems to be what life is about. 'Am I surviving?' is the question she asks even though she has no language. 'Am I getting my way?'

Let us hope she is receiving great love at this time from her parents, who are steadily training her to behave as they want and feel she ought to behave according to a regular routine. Relationships develop and deepen, the child is responsive and good, and with luck the magic line 'Am I loved?' replaces 'Am I surviving?' The child loves in return and wants to please and, beginning to think, thinks of her parents and siblings, if she has any.

For a few lucky children these are the best years, crucial years, still entirely dependent, yet trained, considerate, secure, loved and loving; developing all the time, holding your hand, giving you kisses, calling your name, talking, laughing, full of mischief and fun.

'Am I loved?' Such is emotional survival, but school beckons and when school comes these years will be gone. Suddenly, life really is about survival. No longer kill or be killed as in our caveman's time but a similar kind of terror, albeit caused by a different kind of risk. The danger comes not from animal predators but from other children, older, stronger and bigger, less kind, understanding and caring, than those the child has previously known, demanding, bullying, threatening, ridiculing, aggressive. Such is physical survival.

Then there are the others, less combative but equally forceful in their influence and pressures. Everyone has to conform to a craze, a style, a fad, to a fashion for certain shoes, a certain satchel, in how they speak, what they say, how they present themselves, to in-jokes, to the music, TV, movies they like, in how they dance, how they study, eventually to alcohol, drugs, parties, sex. Such is social survival.

And more pressure builds up. It's all about wealth, where holidays are taken and how often, toys, bicycles, the make and number of cars a family has, the size of houses and gardens, the parents' jobs, kitchen devices, whether the child has a TV in her bedroom, a smartphone, a tablet, a laptop, a computer, an Xbox. Such is material survival.

And crossing these differing forms of survival, these quasi-tribal bondings between children, is another kind of bonding that unites them in rejecting others in the playground, because they are poor, or have different coloured hair or eyes or skin, or are of a different religion or race, because they have spots or are small, eat strange food or are just different. This, too, is a perceived form of survival, emphasising an innate desire of the many for everyone to be the same, considering any deviation of the norm to be a threat to the survival of the many.

None of this is very edifying. It describes the jungle that is the playground, intensified by social media, whether it includes the child who left home on her first day of school asking 'Am I loved?' or the Unborn Child, now of school age, who has no memory of his brief, glorious wisdom. The point to be made here is serious. The playground brings an overwhelming influence to bear on every child during their formative years. During those years everyone is forced to learn how best to survive and the very process of surviving will often change a person completely from the child who first went to school.

Lessons are learned, innocence is lost, pain is experienced, and major compromises are made. Bonds are formed, beliefs and social conventions are shared and the parameters of adult life are set.

The children from the playground become adults in the course of time. The playground has been their survival school and the lessons they have learned from it become the lessons of life. Beliefs, aspirations and prejudices acquired in the playground do not easily change. 'Am I surviving?' becomes a clarion call for each generation. Everyone is groomed in social and material survival, imbued with similar values, style and bias.

And what of 'Am I loved?' What of emotional survival, what of our need as emotional beings to assess our experiences by reference to whether they make us feel loved? What of making ourselves loveable to receive love in return? What of living according to Nature's Morality, giving more to life and relationships to get more back? What of feeling fulfilled and complete, surviving emotionally for the better protection of our genes and, most poignantly, of ourselves? What of finally being at ease in our being?

Unless groomed very firmly in pre-school years to ask 'Am I loved?' it is likely that a child will succumb to the peer pressure that rules the playground. On reaching adulthood this will prove hard to change.

Such is western society. Such is modern life, where the prevailing sadness is periodically vented in public displays of emotion as happened with the death of Princess Diana. This, sadly, is how life is when the majority of people ask 'Am I surviving?' and concentrate their entire existence on trying to survive rather than seeking to live, on pursuing survival for survival's sake rather than fulfilling their need to be loved.

It is no wonder that we all lack maturity in emotional terms. Our ignorance of what our emotions are for and our inability to handle them have rendered us unable to control or to understand our lives.

Now let us consider Salman Rushdie's wry observation: 'This may be the curse of the human race. Not that we are so different from one another. But that we are so alike.' We are indeed alike in our frailties, whether we be presidents or terrorists, parents or children, saints or sinners, oligarchs or peasants. All of us, however grand, however humble, are indeed the same from the way we are built to our lack of ease and our inability to understand or control our emotions. We have the same capacity to love, the same need to be loved, the same wants, dreams and passions, the same desires, the same need to survive and procreate.

That, together with our diversity, is what, miraculously, makes up Humankind.

And that is why the conclusions we have reached, applying as they do to every single human being, holding out the promise of a better, more stable, more loving, more fulfilling existence, are vital to us all.

'O brave new world!' Miranda's explosion of innocence and delight at her first sighting of other human beings must rank as one of the most joyous and exuberant of human reactions. It is surely one that is appropriate for ourselves as we can finally imagine a life better understood and a more loving and much more stable future.

It is a mark of our cohesion as a species that, to conclude our study, we should move on from a fictitious character, the epitome of naivety and innocence, to a real person, one who could not be more different, responsible for calamitous changes to the modern world. 'The philosophers have only interpreted the world in various ways; the point is to change it,' wrote Karl Marx. Well, he was right in so far as he makes our point, namely that contemplating a new and exciting existence for us all, in which our dysfunction will yield to our new understanding, our ignorance of the human condition to our new knowledge, leaving us comfortable in our lives and at ease in our nature, is absolutely the image of a Brave New World.

We can now feel complete. It is not just the vision that can change the world, but the reasoning behind it. For, now that we at last understand the human condition, our world can no longer remain the same. It has to change in emotional and philosophical terms and in a host of different ways. We now understand the protections for Life, the dynamics of Life, the purpose of Life, the reasons for our emotions, the prime importance of love and the all-powerful influence it maintains over human existence, the fact and purpose of our Supreme Sense, the promise of harmony in conducting our lives in accordance to Nature's Morality.

Rushdie is right. We are, all of us, exactly the same. The

only difference between us that really matters is the question we ask through our Supreme Sense. We understand the cost of asking the wrong question and the huge differences we can make to our lives and those of the people we love and interact with, by asking the right one.

Our prospects for a peaceful and fulfilling life have improved dramatically. We know now how we can reach our potential and be happy. Even if it takes a hundred years, our new understanding must change the world for the better.

Epilogue

If it be true that good wine needs no bush,
'tis true that a good play needs no epilogue.
WILLIAM SHAKESPEARE (1564–1616)
As You Like It (1599), Epilogue

As I might have expected, despite a spurt in my final writing, the third act of our opera has indeed duly arrived before the completion of this book. And so, with much pleasure, I produce its synopsis here.

Act 3
Scene 1: God's Celestial Palace

It is night-time, the world is asleep, as Nature visits God. Life, she reports, is wretched with sadness. Humankind is not flourishing and is beginning to fight wars over God. She pleads: is there nothing that can be done to bring the two of them together and grant them happiness? After all, with Life so precious to Nature and Humankind so beloved of God, surely they have a common interest in finding a solution?

'What can I do?' God responds. 'My gift to Humankind when he married Life was freewill.'

Much disturbed, God and Nature join together to sing of their children's distress, the melody of their duet having been introduced as the scene began.

'What can I do?' God laments. 'If only there was Love.'

Nature echoes in response. 'If only there was Love.'

Scene 2: Humankind's House

Humankind and Life are together but all is not well.

Humankind either spends his time with God or fighting over him. He finds no time for Life. Life no longer sees the point of them staying together. 'Am I loved?' she demands.

'Well, you are my wife,' Humankind answers.

'No!' Life pleads. 'I am meant to be your beloved. Beloved means being loved. Love is essential to my survival but I am not loved by you.'

The fight continues. Humankind looks at the large clock on the wall as it strikes three. 'I have to go,' he proclaims. 'I have to go to my Father.'

He leaves at once as Life collapses in tears.

Scene 3: God's Celestial Palace

God and Nature are rebuking Humankind for neglecting Life when, to the sound of trumpets, the grand doors at the rear of the salon suddenly open to a procession of angels carrying a golden throne aloft on which sits Love, dressed in a white robe.

God, Nature and Humankind cease singing as Love's throne is placed on the ground. Bowing low to God, she approaches. Her beauty is breath-taking, and Humankind, who has never seen her like this, is captivated, as if in a spell. God and Nature take each of her hands as Humankind falls to his knees.

At that moment Life enters. She is very sad, having come in great distress, her eyes passing from Humankind, to Love and God and Nature, then back to Humankind again. Seeing Humankind like this, on his knees before his father, touches Life's heart.

The trumpets sound again. The angels approach Life and gently lead her to God, before whom she kneels, next to Humankind. With great solemnity God joins their two hands together. Humankind and Life regard each other with tears in their eyes as Love removes her crown, holding it above the couple's heads. United at last, Life and Humankind fall on each other's necks and fondly embrace.

God and Nature sing a blessing to Life and Humankind as they withdraw.

The opera concludes in a joyous trio of Life, Love and Humankind pledging each other eternal devotion.

This, indeed, is a far more positive ending than previously, made possible by the greater understanding that we now have of our emotions and love, our need to be loved and the human condition. And, yes, we have hope, and, more to the point, we have reason to hope, for a better, more meaningful and fulfilling life in the future.

All that remains is to apply what we have learned to everyday life.

After all that we have examined, it seems right that our final words should be about the very first people to inhabit our world, Adam and Eve.

Taken from Mark Twain's delightful 'Eve's Diary', Eve's prayer, as the first wife, is a song of love. The fruit of all that can grow between two people from loving each other and being loved in return, it reads like an eternal kiss. How appropriate for us to leave each other with this:

> It is my prayer, it is my longing, that we may pass from this life together – a longing which shall never perish from the earth, but shall have place in the hearts of every wife that loves, until the end of time; and it shall be called by my name.
>
> But if one of us must go first, it is my prayer that it shall be I; for he is strong, I am weak, I am not so necessary to him as he is to me – life without him would not be life; how could I endure it? This prayer is also immortal, and will not cease from being offered up while my race continues. I am the first wife; and in the last wife I shall be repeated.

At Eve's grave
ADAM: Wheresoever she was, there was Eden.

APPENDIX

A Selection of Thoughts

Each generation starts from scratch.

The human body is of impossibly intricate complexity, involving miles of tubing, acres of membranes, ten times more bacteria than our trillions of cells and, it is said, enough blood pumped through us in our lifetime to fill the Royal Albert Hall.

In terms of evolution our faculties are revolutionary; our real problem is that we have yet to learn how to use them.

One degree of misunderstanding may not appear to be very much, but one degree is the difference in DNA between chimpanzees and ourselves. It is enough to produce an entirely different animal. So it is with misunderstandings, which have left human beings so far from their true potential.

Each day a man would pass through customs on the border between countries A and B, wheeling his bicycle, a box of sand attached in a frame behind the saddle. Each day the man would wait patiently whilst the border guards checked the sand, searching through it with their hands, once even sending a sample for analysis.

Each day the border guards found nothing.

This procedure continued for many months until, with the coming of Christmas, the border guards relaxed their formality. 'We know you're smuggling something,' the senior officer said. 'Tell us what it is and we won't charge you.'

The man looked amazed, his eyes passing from one guard to the other, but he said nothing.

'Come on, just tell us,' the senior officer repeated. 'It's Christmas. We'll let you off.'

The man appeared to hesitate, then, sighing deeply, he mounted his bicycle. 'I don't know what you're talking about,' he said. But from that day on he gave up smuggling bicycles.

It's human nature. The border guards never gave the bicycle a thought. And so it is with ourselves. We constantly search through the box of sand, which is our life, the human condition, the complexity of our existence on this earth, but we pay little attention to that which protects our life, the bicycle in our story that carries the box of sand.

We are concerned with an entire species, the first and so far the only emotional beings, multi-talented, massively intelligent, capable of huge discoveries and great inventions, of creating civilisation and magnificent works of art, dominating the earth and all that is in it, of communicating in a multitude of languages and living in a raft of different cultures, yet we are a species strangely ill at ease in its nature, unable to live life free of sadness, misery, confusion, despair, unable to find fulfilment.

'Life is something to do when you can't get to sleep.'

FRAN LEBOWITZ (b. 1950)

Having been selected for life from between 400 and 500 million rivals, one would have thought that we would emerge from nine months of warmth, good food and security as winners, all cocky and confident and ready to take on the world. Not so. One thing that our emotions and superior brains have given us, distinguishing us from all other animals, is a permanent feeling of insecurity.

If you remove affluence from the recipe for happiness then our way of life makes no sense.

Nature provides the need to be loved to protect Life within us, and we give it to God.

If the greatest need is to be loved, the greatest concern is whether we are loved.

Feeling loved is the only way we can ultimately feel whole and happy and fulfilled, at peace with ourselves and at one with our emotions.

Needing someone to love us is a major pre-occupation of humanity.

> 'I thought love would adapt itself to my needs.
> But needs grow too fast;
> They come up like weeds
> Through cracks in the conversation,
> Through silences in the dark
> Through everything you thought was concrete.'
> ALICE WALKER (b. 1949), 'Did This Happen to your
> Mother? Did Your Sister Throw Up a Lot?' (1979)

Our Supreme Sense engenders the core feeling which we use to interact with the world around us, making it a personal world, creating our private sense of self and identity. This is how we view and experience every single sensation we are ever exposed to, in a continual assessment of the degree to which we feel loved and are surviving.

Our ignorance of the human condition has restricted us in all our actions, all our thoughts and plans, providing half-people, unaware of the treasure that we carry within us.

'Our conscious minds hunger for a permanent existence. If we cannot have everlasting life of the body, then absorption into some immortal soul will serve. Anything will serve as long as it gives the individual meaning and somehow stretches into eternity.'

E. O. WILSON (b. 1929)

'Death followed by Eternity... the worst of both worlds.'

TOM STOPPARD (b. 1937),
Rosencrantz and Guildenstern Are Dead (1966), Act 2

'He saw it as irresponsibly hopeful to imagine a better world existed after this one, in some unnamed, unknown, unproved plane of existence. As foolish as it was to believe that this is the best of all possible worlds, said Professor Jove, it was a thousand times more foolish to believe in a best possible Afterworld.'

SHALOM AUSLANDER (b. 1970), *Hope: A Tragedy* (2012)

'We are miserable enough in this life,
without the absurdity of speculating upon
another.'

LORD BYRON (1788–1824)

'God is love, but get it in writing.'
GYPSY ROSE LEE (1911–70)

'Unbelievers turn the *hoc est corpus meum*
of the Eucharist into "hocus pocus".'

ROY PORTER (1946–2002),
Flesh in the Age of Reason (2003)

'Someone has somewhere commented on the fact that
millions long for immortality who don't know what
to do with themselves on a rainy Sunday afternoon.'

SUSAN ERTZ (1887–1985), *Anger in the Sky* (1943)

'Whatever a man prays for, he prays for a miracle.
Every prayer reduces itself to this: Great God, grant
that twice two be not four.'

IVAN TURGENEV (1818–83), 'Prayer' (1881)

Bibliography

The Passages on Pages 98 and 99 from *Cyrano de Bergerac*, translated by Anthony Burgess, are quoted by permission of the publisher, Nick Hern Books.

Appleyard, Bryan: *How to Live Forever or Die Trying: On the New Immortality* (2007) Simon and Schuster

Armstrong, Karen: *A History of God* (1994) Mandarin

—— *The Battle for God: A History of Fundamentalism* (2001) Ballantine

Becker, Gavin de: *The Gift of Fear: Survival Signals That Protect Us from Violence* (1997) Bloomsbury

Behe, Michael J.: *The Edge of Evolution: The Search for the Limits of Darwinism* (2007) Free Press

Bloom, Harold: *The Book of J* (1991) Faber and Faber

Bryson, Bill: *A Short History of Nearly Everything* (2003) Doubleday

Citron, Lana: *A Compendium of Kisses* (2010) Beautiful Books

Cole, Jonathan: *About Face* (1998) Bradford

Damasio, Antonio: *The Feeling of What Happens: Body, Emotions and the Making of Consciousness* (1999) William Heinemann

Dawkins, Richard: *The Selfish Gene* (1976) Oxford University Press

—— *The Blind Watchmaker* (1986) Penguin

—— *Unweaving the Rainbow: Science, Delusion and the Appetite for Wonder* (1998) Allen Lane

—— *The Ancestor's Tale: A Pilgrimage to the Dawn of Life* (2004) Weidenfeld and Nicolson

—— *The God Delusion* (2006) Bantam Press

Dennett, Daniel C.: *Breaking the Spell: Religion as a Natural Phenomenon* (2006) Allen Lane

Edelman, Gerald M.: *Wider than the Sky: The Phenomenal Gift of Consciousness* (2004) Allen Lane

Frayn, Michael: *The Human Touch: Our Part in the Creation of a Universe* (2006) Faber and Faber

Goleman, Daniel: *Emotional Intelligence: Why It Can Matter More than IQ* (1995) Bantam Press

Gray, John: *False Dawn: The Delusions of Global Capitalism* (1998) Granta

—— *Straw Dogs: Thoughts on Humans and Other Animals* (2002) Granta

—— *Black Mass: Apocalyptic Religion and the Death of Utopia* (2007) Allen Lane

Greenfield, Susan A.: *The Human Brain: A Guided Tour* (1997) Weidenfeld and Nicolson

—— *The Private Life of the Brain* (2000) Allen Lane

Harris, John: *Clones, Genes and Immortality: Ethics and the Genetic Revolution* (1992) Oxford University Press

Hawking, Stephen W.: *A Brief History of Time: From the Big Bang to Black Holes* (1998) Bantam Press

Himmelfarb, Gertrude: *The Moral Imagination: From Edmund Burke to Lionel Trilling* (2007) Souvenir Press

Hitchens, Christopher: *God Is Not Great: The Case against Religion* (2007) Atlantic

Humphrey, Nicholas: *The History of the Mind* (1993) Vintage

Jones, Steve: *The Language of the Genes* (1994) Flamingo

—— *In the Blood: God, Genes and Destiny* (1997) Flamingo

LeDoux, Joseph: *The Emotional Brain: The Mysterious Underpinnings of Emotional Life* (1998) Weidenfeld and Nicolson

Lewis, Thomas, Fari Amini and Richard Lannon: *A General Theory of Love* (2001) Vintage

McGrath, Alister E.: *The Dawkins Delusion: Atheist Fundamentalism and the Denial of the Divine* (2007) Society for Promoting Christian Knowledge

183

Maddox, John: *What Remains to Be Discovered? Mapping the Secrets of the Universe, the Origins of Life, and the Future of the Human Race* (1997) Free Press

Midgley, Mary: *Science and Poetry* (2001) Routledge

Pinker, Steven: *The Language Instinct: The New Science of Language and Mind* (1994) Allen Lane

—— *How the Mind Works* (1997) Allen Lane

—— *The Blank Slate: The Modern Denial of Human Nature* (2002) Penguin. Allen Lane

—— *The Stuff of Thought: Language as a Window into Human Nature* (2007) Allen Lane

Pollock, Frederick: *Spinoza: His Life and Philosophy* ([1880] 2010) Kessinger

Porter, Roy: *Flesh in the Age of Reason* (2003) Allen Lane

Revel, Jean-François and Matthieu Ricard: *The Monk and the Philosopher: East Meets West in a Father–Son Dialogue* (1999) Thorsons

Ridley, Matt: Genome: *The Autobiography of a Species in 23 Chapters* (1999) Fourth Estate

—— *Nature via Nurture: Genes, Experience and What Makes Us Human* (2003) Fourth Estate

Rose, Hilary and Steven Rose: *Alas Poor Darwin: Arguments against Evolutionary Psychology* (2001) Vintage

Sacks, Jonathan: *Faith in the Future* (1995) Darton, Longman and Todd

Safina, Carl: *Beyond Words: What Animals Think and Feel* (2016) Souvenir Press

Spinoza, Benedict: *Ethics* ([1677] 1996) Penguin

Wilson, Edward O.: *Consilience: The Unity of Knowledge* (1998) Little, Brown

Winston, Robert: *Human Instinct* (2002) Bantam Press

Acknowledgements

What do I acknowledge? My warmest thanks to all readers for sharing with me the thoughts presented here. I hope your read was worthwhile and that you will long consider what I have enunciated and in so doing benefit from a greater appreciation of life and how we should be able to live it.

I further acknowledge that I was a fool.

You see I allowed myself to be seduced by a firm of publicists in the United States who assured me that this book was a legacy book that would sell for thirty years and go straight to the top of the New York Times best sellers list.

I ask myself whether it had anything to do with the fee I had paid them, after which for over six months I was told this so often that eventually I allowed myself to dare to dream that it was true? Then out of the blue something weird happened. The consultant handling the book, whom I had liked immensely, was suddenly in prison having broken his parole of which I had known nothing, and the Agent he had found for me had a major stroke. And there was no one in the firm able to continue to represent the book in any effective way.

Of course I had been duped, I was a fool for allowing myself to believe what I wanted to believe but then, as I emphasise here, and this is my ultimate consolation, at best all of us are only human.

And so, back in the United Kingdom, I acknowledge my deep gratitude to Umbria Press and my debt to Alan Gordon Walker, my Publisher, to Jonathan Wadman, my Editor and Louise Millar who has designed the book.

As a father it gives me particular pleasure to acknowledge the staunch and devoted support I have received from all my children and to thank particularly Kara Bieber for designing the book cover and Leo Bieber for taking the cover portrait.

I am also delighted to acknowledge my great and warmest thanks to Dr Nick Cooling, Dr Herb Etkin, Bruce Mauleverer QC, Michael Cockerham, Jeremy White, Robert Bergerhoff Mulder, Stephanie Hertzig, Alex Wood, Bethanie Alhadeff, Gaby Fyjus Walker, Emma Gregson-Williams, Michael Brown, Annasue Wilson, Annabelle Mitzman, Baruch Naeh, Shir Naeh, Amalia Arenguren, Hugo Bieber and Lark Lumbroso, all of whom have given me wonderful support.

Finally I acknowledge my deepest thanks to one person above all for her faith and encouragement throughout the gestation of this book (for far longer than the combined gestation of our four children) and for her constant love -- my beloved Joey.

Index